G(

GREA ___ ...IN

A Guide to the Bible

R LLEWELYN WILLIAMS

THE COVENANT PUBLISHING CO. LTD.
121, Low Etherley, Bishop Auckland, Co. Durham, DL14 0HA

2015

Digitally Reproduced
Book

GOD'S GREAT PLAN

A GUIDE TO THE BIBLE

by

R. LLEWELYN WILLIAMS

Author of
The Hope that is in us
The Mystery of the Kingdom of God
Hidden Treasure
etc.

SIXTH EDITION

1973
THE COVENANT PUBLISHING CO., LTD.
6 Buckingham Gate, S.W.1

First published	1939
Second Edition	1940
Third Edition	1941
Fourth Edition	1947
Fifth Edition	1958
Sixth Edition	1973
Seventh Edition	2007
Reprinted	2015

ISBN 978-0-85205-044-6

CONTENTS

6

FOREWORD

To the inexperienced student the Bible presents itself as a collection of sixty-six books written by a large number of authors, and at first sight this mass of literature may well seem to be merely an Hebrew anthology of little interest to any save the antiquarian. Some time may elapse before such a student discovers that all these books possess a common theme, to which each author makes his own individual contribution.

Even more time may elapse before it is realised that this co-ordination of thought in so many authors, and over so great a period of time, is a work too great for ordinary human intelligence to have achieved.

In these pages, therefore, an attempt has been made to trace that great central theme of the Bible which links all its books together, and which justifies their inclusion in one volume as the Book of Books.

Careful study of the selected passages of Scripture will, it is hoped, lead the student to the conclusion that the Bible is not only a true book, but something of far greater value— the written Word of our Lord and Saviour, Jesus Christ, who is Himself the Living Word of God.

CHAPTER I

IN THE BEGINNING

The Bible

Our gracious King, we present you with this Book, the most valuable thing that this world affords. Here is wisdom; this is the royal law; these are the lively oracles of God.

With these words the Primate of All England presents to the newly-crowned king the first gift of all his loyal subjects, a copy of the Holy Bible.

Truer words were never framed by lips of man. The Bible is, indeed, the most precious thing which this world affords; for it supplies that knowledge which is able to make us wise unto salvation; it contains the books of the Divine Law; and it sets forth God's own revelation of Himself, and of His purpose for all mankind.

Read 2 Timothy iii, 14-17.

God

The process of initiation into the living oracles of God begins with the very first sentence of the Bible: "In the beginning God created the heaven and the earth."

There in the fewest and simplest of words lies the revelation of a Supreme Being, outside the limitations of time and space, who is, in Himself, the source of all energy and power.

The Trinity

The parallel account in the New Testament associates the work of creation very closely with the second person of the Trinity, God the Son.

Read John i, 1-3.

Turning back to the second verse of Genesis, we read that "the Spirit of God moved upon the face of the waters."

Thus, at the very outset of our studies, we find the revelation of the great Triune God—Father, Son and Holy Spirit; Three in One and One in Three.

The Two Creations

In the opening sentence of the Bible the whole history of creation is compressed into one short passage. This passage undoubtedly covers the six divine "days," or epochs of time, during which God created the present world. But it may also embrace even more history than is evident at first sight; for we find in other parts of the Bible indications of a prior creation, which was ruined and wrecked in the mists of antiquity.

Without Form and Void

Lt.-Col. L. Merson Davies, in his wholly admirable book, *The Bible and Modern Science*, states on p. 89: "It is a notable fact, which has been pointed out times without number, that there is a totally indefinite gap between the first two verses of Genesis. Nor is this all; for the language of the second verse further implies that it does not at all refer to a primitive condition of the world, but to a late and ruined condition."

For an explanation of this "gap," he refers us to the book of Jeremiah.

Read Genesis i, 1-2; Jeremiah iv, 23-26.

Col. Davies then continues, on p. 103: "Now this is the only other passage in the whole Bible in which the identical words 'tohu va-bohu' (rendered "without form and void") of Genesis i, 2 reappear; and the connection here is with a wrecked and ruined world which has been the habitation of man, but whose heavenly lights have been withdrawn under the judgment of God. So if this passage does nothing else it clearly shows, as Skinner himself allows (*A Critical and Exegetical Commentary on Genesis*, pp. 16-17), that the 'safest' way of regarding the second verse of Genesis is to take it as representing a 'darkened and devastated earth, from which life and order have fled.'

"We could hardly, therefore, have a better warrant for so taking it. If, as a critic like Skinner admits, this view is the 'safest,' it is surely the one which cautious exegesis should accept before any other."

Darkness

This disaster is closely connected with darkness, or absence of light, both in Jeremiah and Genesis.

Scientists inform us that the withdrawal of the light and heat of the sun would result in such appalling cold that the whole world would be reduced to a frozen waste in which all forms of life would cease to exist.

Commenting on this, Col. Davies points out that "tohu" is the very word which is used in Job to describe the frozen waste around the North Pole.

Read Job xxvi, 7.

Throughout the Bible darkness is closely associated with evil. When, therefore, we read that this disaster was the result of the fierce anger of the Lord, we can only suppose that it was provoked by the evil of the inhabitants of the cities of the earth.

Satan

The earliest manifestation of evil for which we have any record is described in the last book of the Bible, where we read that the great red dragon, that old serpent called the Devil and Satan, makes war on his Creator, and is cast out into the earth with all his following of angels.

Read Revelation xii, 7-9.

That Satan before his fall was an archangel of great wisdom, beauty and power, is evident from the description which is given of him as the spiritual power behind the throne of the king of Tyre.

Read Ezekiel xxviii, 11-19.

From the book of Isaiah we learn that it was pride in all this beauty and wisdom and power which fired Satan with the ambition to seize the throne of God Himself.

Read Isaiah xiv, 12-14.

Evil

Thus we are given to understand that the unfathomable mystery of iniquity originated in the spiritual sphere, and manifested itself in rebellion against God.

11

The Fallen Angels

For this crime, as we have already seen, Satan was cast out into the earth, and all his following of angels with him.

That this following was a mighty host cannot be doubted; for we read that the great red dragon's tail "drew the third part of the stars of heaven, and did cast them to the earth."

In their fallen state these angels are closely associated with darkness, and, in fact, become the powers and rulers of the darkness of this world.

Read Revelation xii, 3-4; Jude 6; Ephesians vi, 12.

Satan's Ambition

The Bible makes it very clear that, in spite of his fall, Satan remained a spirit of great power, and that he still retained his ambition to defeat the purposes of God. This ambition is expressed in the words, "I will sit also upon the mount of the congregation in the sides of the North."

If we turn to the Book of Psalms we shall find these words: "Great is the Lord, and greatly to be praised in the city of our God, in the *mountain of His holiness*. Beautiful for situation, the joy of the whole earth, is Mount Zion, *on the sides of the North*, the city of the great king."

So it would appear that, from very early times, Satan has cherished the design of usurping the Kingdom of God on earth, and of reigning over the whole world from Jerusalem.

Read Psalm xlviii, 1-3.

The Prince of this World

Satan's exact powers, after his fall, are not clearly defined, although we may gather from the book of Job some idea of his privileged position.

Read Job i, 6-12.

At the same time, it may fairly be inferred that, while he was yet an angel of light, he was placed in charge of the earth as an agent of God, and that, even after his fall, this privilege was not entirely withdrawn. For even after a lapse of many thousands of years, we find him arrogantly asserting his claims to be the Prince of this World, and, moreover, making that claim to God the Son, who was Himself the Creator of the Universe.

Read Luke iv, 5-8.

It should be noted that Jesus did not refute this claim; indeed, had He done so, the Devil's proposal would not have been the terrible temptation which it undoubtedly was.

On the contrary, Jesus tacitly admitted the claim, and rebuked him with a quotation from the Mosaic Law.

Nor is this all; for on at least three occasions Jesus gave him the title of "The Prince of this World."

Read John xii, 31; xiv, 30; xvi, 11.

Satan and the Disaster

Our examination of the accounts of Satan's downfall has already shown us that this was the direct consequence of rebellion against the will of God. Further examination discloses the fact that both versions imply, if they do not actually state, that one phase of this rebellion was the deception, or weakening, of the nations of the whole world.

Thus we read in Revelation xii, 9: "Satan, which deceiveth the whole world; he was cast out into the earth"; and in Isaiah xiv, 12: "How art thou cut down to the ground, which didst weaken the nations!"

Bearing in mind that, when Satan makes his appearance on the scene in Genesis iii, he is already a fallen angel, we are led to the conclusion that the disaster which befell the prior creation was due in no small measure to his agency.

If, as the name implies, Lucifer's commission was to bring light—both physical light and the light of the knowledge of God—to the world, then abuse of his commission, resulting in the demoralisation of the nations, would bring upon the world that disastrous darkness to which we have already referred.

Assuming, then, that the argument for a prior creation is well founded, we may now arrange these far-off events in their probable sequence by reading the relative passages in the following order.

Read John i, 1-3; Genesis i, 1; Job xxxviii, 4-7; Revelation xii, 7-9; Ezekiel xxviii, 12-19; Isaiah xiv, 12-14; Jeremiah iv, 23-26; Genesis i, 2.

13

CHAPTER II

THE CREATION OF THIS WORLD

The Seven Days

From verse 3 the first chapter of Genesis records the creation (or recreation), of this present world in seven successive stages:

(1) Light. Day and night.
(2) Atmosphere. Water upon the earth. Water surrounding the earth, outside the atmosphere.
(3) Dry land. Vegetation.
(4) Sun, moon, planets and stars.
(5) Fish. Fowl.
(6) Beasts of the field. Human beings.
(7) Rest.

Read Genesis i, 3—ii, 3.

Adam and Eve

The second chapter of Genesis records the creation of Adam and Eve. Whether they were, or were not, the first man and woman of this present creation, as distinct from the prior creation, is a matter of some controversy.

One school of thought postulates the existence of human beings in this present creation before Adam and Eve.

It is pointed out that man and woman were created in the Sixth Stage, and that the creation of Adam is recorded after the Seventh Stage, or Day of Rest.

It is further pointed out that Eve was created some time after Adam, whereas there is nothing to indicate that man and woman in the Sixth Stage were not created simultaneously.

It is also demonstrated that between the record of the creation of man and woman in the Sixth Stage, and of the creation of Adam and Eve, we find the statement that "there was not a man to till the ground." And it is claimed, quite reasonably, that this may be interpreted as meaning that there were already men upon the earth, but that none of them had up to that time begun to practise husbandry.

As this view is not out of harmony with the Biblical record, we may adopt it for the sake of argument, and see whither it will lead us.

If we suppose that human beings existed in the present creation before Adam and Eve, then we must admit that they were created beings of a very exalted order indeed; for we are told that they were made in the image and likeness of God; and we are also told that God gave to them "dominion over every living thing that moveth upon the earth."

Having admitted this, we are immediately confronted by certain difficulties, which may be put in the form of questions.

(1) Wherein lay the necessity for a special creation of Adam, who is also described in the recapitulation in Genesis v, 1-2 as made "in the likeness of God"?

(2) Why was it necessary to create again "every beast of the field and every fowl of the air," as described in Genesis ii, 19, when these forms of life had already been created in the Fifth and Sixth Stages?

(3) How could the sin of one man, created in the likeness of God, involve all his contemporaries, also created in the likeness of God, in the consequences of his downfall?

The Traditional View

Without attempting to answer these questions, we would venture to suggest that the creation of Adam and Eve which is recorded in Genesis ii, is an amplification, or detailed description, of the creation of man and woman which is recorded in Genesis i.

This is the traditional view; its reasonableness is confirmed by the second recapitulation of the creation in Genesis v, 1-2, and by the description of Eve as "the mother of all living."

The Excellence of Creation

At each stage of creation, except the Second where the words are omitted, we read that "God saw that it was good"; and when it was all finished, "God saw everything that He had made, and, behold, it was very good."

This emphatic insistence upon the "goodness" of the creation is evidently intended to impress upon our minds a great truth.

When we consider the world in which we find ourselves to-day, we realise that it is a world marred by sin and death. It is not, therefore, in all respects the same world as that which was originally created. For if God could say that everything which He had made was very good, then we can only suppose that it must have been perfect.

Peace

Over all this creation reigned that peace which springs from perfect harmony with the will of God. The lower orders of the living world were at peace in themselves and also with man; man himself was at peace with God.

Fear had no place in the Garden of Eden; for hunger and pain and death were not yet known.

Made in the Likeness of God

Perfect in physique, perfect in intellect, Adam and Eve walked and talked as friends with the source of all knowledge and power. Wisdom and happiness were theirs beyond our understanding.

The First Covenant

With this man and woman God made a Covenant, the first of the eight great Covenants of the Bible (Genesis i, 26-30). Only one condition was imposed, the exercise of their free will in accordance with the command of their Creator.

One thing in particular was forbidden—the knowledge of, or acquaintance with, evil. For this, as they were warned, would be disastrous to their happiness, and would, indeed, bring about a change in their bodies from an immortal to a mortal condition (Genesis ii, 16-17).

The Divine Purpose

From this, and from the general tenor of the Bible, it is evident that God envisaged a perfect race living in a perfect world, where sin and misery were unknown.

It was to be a place of abundance for man and beast; a place of perfect health and happiness; a place of peace, where no man oppressed his brother; and a place where God was the only king.

Read Genesis ii, 4-25.

CHAPTER III

THE FALL OF MAN

The Temptation

Into this paradise on earth came Satan, hot with rebellion against God, and burning to defeat His purposes. How was he to gain his ends, and satisfy the desire of his soul for the worship of all mankind?

Before him were the father and mother of all the future race. If he could seduce them from their allegiance to God, if he could infect them with the poison of evil, he could ruin God's wonderful creation and at the same time lay the foundations of his own kingdom over the hearts of men.

With this purpose in view he approached Eve, no doubt posing as an Angel of Light, and proceeded to sow the first germ of doubt in her mind: "Are you quite sure that God told you not to grasp at greater knowledge than that which you already possess?"

To which Eve replied in effect: "God has warned us that if we even attempt to do so, we shall lose our immortal bodies, and become subject to death."

"But," insinuated Satan, "greater knowledge would only make you more like God; He knows that very well. Of course you would not die. You and Adam are made in the image and likeness of God, and you are very wonderful. But you can make yourselves even more wonderful; you can acquire knowledge, and knowledge is power. With all this knowledge and power you can be as good as gods yourselves."

The Lie

The Devil succeeded in his temptation by inventing that terrible lie, "ye shall not surely die." This is the first and greatest lie of all history; this is THE LIE of all lies, the cause of all our troubles, and the root of all disbelief.

It deceived Eve, and it deceived Adam. They poisoned themselves with evil, and thus brought upon themselves the consequence of death; not immediate physical death, for Adam lived till he was 930 years old, but ultimate death, physical and spiritual, not only for their own bodies and souls, but for those of all their posterity.

Read Genesis iii, 1-13.

The Second Covenant

As the First Covenant had been broken, God made with Adam a Second Covenant, which consisted mainly of a curse, but nevertheless held out the promise of a future blessing.

The Curse

Because they had disobeyed the voice of God, because they had deliberately contaminated themselves with evil, Adam and Eve were banished from the garden. They forfeited the ideal existence of Eden, and brought upon themselves the punishment of the curse: toil and sorrow, pain and death.

In these changed circumstances it became necessary for man to work, and work hard, to maintain an existence, the continuance of which was sorrow, and the end of which was death.

Since that time all human beings have been born in a state of degradation and sin. Thus, when the Psalmist says, "Behold, I was shapen in iniquity; and in sin did my mother conceive me" (Psalm li, 5), he is simply stating that he, like all other human beings, was born in a state of degradation which was caused by Adam's disobedience.

Read Genesis iii, 14-24.

In some way, which is difficult to understand, Adam's fall involved the whole of the natural creation. Not only

18

was the ground cursed for his sake, but all the living creatures upon it.

From St. Paul we learn that "the whole creation groaneth and travaileth in pain together"; while Isaiah, in a vision of the future, foretells the ultimate restoration of the beasts of the field to their original state of harmony with the will of God.

Read Romans viii, 18-23; Isaiah xi, 6-9.

Responsibility for the Curse

Possibly no error is more widespread than that which blames God for the curse, and ascribes to Him the pain, and the sorrow, and the suffering which are all too evident in our midst.

This error is largely due to the false doctrine of Evolution, which denies both the creation and the fall. But the Bible leaves us in no doubt that the curse is the work of Satan; and for this we have the confirmation of God the Son Himself.

Read John viii, 43-45.

The Greek words, $\tau \grave{o} \ \psi \epsilon \hat{v} \delta o \varsigma$, which occur in the above passage, are translated "*a* lie"; but the literal translation is "*the* lie."

Thus when our Lord states, in the same breath, that the Devil was a murderer *from the beginning*, we realise that the lie to which He refers is THE LIE by which Satan became the murderer of the whole human race.

The Love of God

Let us beware lest we presume to sit in judgment upon the Judge of all the earth. God had warned Adam and Eve of the danger of meddling with forbidden things, much as a mother may warn her child not to play with fire. If the child is disobedient and burns itself, the mother is not to blame; her heart is grieved, but her love remains.

Shall we ascribe to God a love inferior to that of a human being? Surely not. Just as a mother would set about the task of restoring her child to health, so we may imagine God formed His plan for restoring man to his original state of innocence.

19

How was this to be done? Could God, while forgiving man his sin, cancel the consequences of his folly? A moment's reflection will be sufficient to convince us that this would have been impossible, for two reasons.

Firstly, because God is a changeless and consistent Being who never breaks His word; indeed, were it otherwise, it would be impossible to trust Him.

Secondly, because God had given to man the gift of free will, and this He could not take away without reducing him to a state of slavery.

Was there, then, no way by which man, of his own free will, might regain that which he had lost?

God's Great Plan for Salvation

There was one way; a way so staggering, so tremendous that man still jeers at its apparent impossibility.

That way was to be what the Epistle to the Hebrews (x, 20) describes as "a new and living way." God Himself in the person of God the Son, the Creator of the world and the Maker of its laws, was to lay aside His divine powers; become man, mortal man as Adam was after his fall; subject Himself to the same, or greater, temptations; take upon Himself the sins, past, present and future, of the whole world; pay the inevitable penalty of death; and so buy back, redeem, for man all those blessings which man himself had forfeited.

The Promise

Thus we find in the Second Covenant the promise of a Saviour, "the seed of the woman," who should reverse the destructive work of Satan.

Later, as we shall see, the Saviour is born of woman, and is hailed by John the Baptist as "the Lamb of God, which taketh away the sin of the world."

During His mortal life the Saviour makes His great announcements: "I am THE WAY. The Son of Man is come to seek and to save that which was lost. I am come that they might have LIFE, and that they might have it more abundantly."

After His ascension, the Saviour reveals Himself as "the Lamb slain from the foundation of the world."

Read Genesis iii, 14-15; John i, 29: xiv, 6; Luke xix, 10; John x, 10; Revelation xiii, 8; John iii, 16-17.

This is the very pith and marrow of God's Great Plan of Salvation. This is the answer of the Bible to those so-called scholars who presume to criticise their Creator. This is the retort of the Word of God to the Modernists and the Evolutionists, who bleat in unison, "How can we believe in the cruel, vengeful God of the Old Testament?"

God so loved the world that He gave His only-begotten Son; and the Son was not only given, but gave Himself in the Garden of Eden, if not before.

CHAPTER IV

THE GREAT FLOOD

Cain and Seth

Very little time elapsed before evil began to manifest itself in the form of crime. Cain, Adam's eldest son, murdered his own brother Abel, and "went out from the presence of the Lord." By this felony he forfeited his birthright, which was bestowed on his younger brother, Seth.

Read Genesis iv, 1-16; iv, 25-26.

The Line of Seth

Although no hint is given in the Bible of Adam's remorse, this must have been a weary burden; for he lived to see eight generations of his descendants sink deeper and deeper into degradation and sin.

Nevertheless there was preserved throughout this time an unbroken line of God-fearing men, whose names are recorded in the fifth chapter of Genesis. And it is interesting to note that Adam lived to see Lamech, the father of Noah, grow up to manhood.

The World before the Flood

One thousand six hundred and eighty-six years elapsed between the Fall of Adam and the Flood; and during this time the population of the world must have attained considerable dimensions.

Some idea of the length of this period may be gained by a simple calculation. If we reckon 1,686 years from the coronation of King George VI, we are taken back to A.D. 251, at which date the Romans were in occupation of this country, and Constantine the Great had not yet been born.

Throughout this era Satan had done his work so well, and man had been such a willing tool, that the moral and physical condition of the world was utterly corrupt. By its very wickedness the human race threatened to destroy itself.

The Great Flood

Drastic action was necessary if the human race was to be preserved; and God determined to use a great flood of water for this purpose.

The Annular Theory

Here we may mention an interesting theory which has been put forward in explanation of this unique phenomenon.

The waters which appeared in the Second Stage of creation were divided by the firmament, or atmosphere of the earth. Therefore, the "waters under the firmament" are assumed to be the waters, which then lay upon the face of the earth; while the expression "waters above the firmament" is taken to mean a dense envelope of moisture completely surrounding the earth outside its atmosphere.

In course of time this watery envelope would tend to become flattened by centrifugal force; that is to say, the envelope would be flung farther and farther from the equator, and drawn gradually closer to the poles.

Eventually the accumulated density of water over the polar caps would become so great that the envelope would burst, and an overwhelming deluge would surge in two huge waves from the poles up to the equator, submerging the tops of the highest mountains.

Once the envelope had burst, the more distant parts of it

would fall steadily upon the earth, but with less force. As the deep indentations of the earth's crust filled up, the water would gradually find its own level and leave the upper plateaux high and dry.

Noah

Be that as it may, it was not God's intention that the human race should be utterly destroyed. He therefore selected Noah from all the inhabitants of the earth and commanded him to make an immense ark, or raft, in which he and his family, and representative specimens of the animal world, could float upon the flood until the waters had subsided.

Read Genesis vi; vii; viii, 1-19.

Noah "found grace in the eyes of the Lord" for two reasons.

Noah's Descent

In the first place, he was "perfect in his generations." His genealogy, which is given in Genesis v, shows that he was of pure descent from Seth, and not from the murderer, Cain.

Noah's Faith

In the second place, he was "a just man and walked with God." This implies the possession of great faith; and we find this aspect of his character emphasised in the Epistle to the Hebrews.

Read Genesis vi, 8-9; Hebrews xi, 7.

The Ark

Faith of no common kind was, indeed, necessary for the task to which Noah was called. The building of the Ark was an immense undertaking in itself; while the apparent hopelessness of attempting to ride out the Deluge in a craft of his own construction might well have filled him with despair.

Nevertheless, Noah and his sons obeyed the voice of God. They probably started operations near the edge of some large wood in order to lessen the work of hauling the timber.

23

There may have been a stream or river near by; but as the work progressed, the possibility of launching this huge vessel must have become more and more remote, until at last it became evident that it could only be floated off by some kind of flood.

To Noah's friends and contemporaries the situation must have seemed ludicrous in the extreme; so ludicrous, indeed, that they derided his plans and jeered at his warnings.

The Flood and the Second Advent

The attitude of these men and women is described by our Lord, and compared with the attitude of those who scoff at the very idea of His Second Coming.

St. Peter couples present-day ridicule of the Second Advent with disbelief in the Creation and the Flood, and indicates that the one is the direct outcome of the other.

Read Matthew xxiv, 36-39; 2 Peter iii, 3-7.

The Human Race Preserved

After 150 days the waters began to subside and the Ark came to rest on dry ground. All living creatures had been destroyed with the exception of those within its shelter.

Of all human beings only Noah and his wife, his three sons and their wives, had possessed faith sufficiently strong to ensure their preservation from the Flood, and to give the race a fresh start.

The Third, or Noahic, Covenant

The provisions of the covenant which was made with Noah after the Flood are introduced by the words "while the earth remaineth," and may be summarised as follows:

(1) The promise not to drown the world again.
(2) The establishment or confirmation of the day cycle, the year cycle, and the succession of the seasons.
(3) The guarantee of the food supply.
(4) Man's trusteeship for animal life.
(5) The right to take animal life for food.
(6) The prohibition of the consumption of blood.
(7) The sanctity of human life.

24

(8) The institution of capital punishment for murder.

Read Genesis viii, 20—ix, 17.

Life and Death

With the Great Flood we come to the end of a definite epoch in the age-long struggle between Good and Evil, between Light and Darkness, between Life and Death, between God the Son and Satan.

Read 2 Cor. vi, 14-18; John xii, 44-50.

On the one hand we see Jesus begging and imploring men and women to come to Him, of their own free will, for Light and Life.

On the other hand we see Satan deceiving men and women with lies, and leading them, of their own free will, to Darkness and Death.

All history has been, and is, a reflex of this tremendous spiritual warfare for the souls of men.

Read Ephesians vi, 11-13.

CHAPTER V

ABRAHAM AND ISAAC

Nimrod

Depressed though Satan may have been by the obliteration of his kingdom, he was soon busily engaged in setting up another; and he found a tool ready to his hand in Nimrod, the mighty hunter, whose name means "the rebel."

Nimrod, great-grandson of Noah, was probably the first man, after the Flood, to establish himself as a sovereign ruler over his fellow-men, and to make organised warfare upon neighbouring countries. He was also a builder of cities, the most famous of which were Babylon and Nineveh.

The Tower of Babel

According to Josephus, the Jewish historian, he persuaded his people that it was weakness and foolishness on their part to put their trust in God, and vowed that he would build a tower so strong and so high that no flood could ever submerge it.

That tower, the Tower of Babel, although never completed, was actually built, and stood for centuries—a symbol of his arrogant defiance.

Read Genesis x, 8-12; xi, 1-9.

Babylon

Here, then, in Babylon, Satan enthroned himself as the Prince of this World. Here he was worshipped as Baal, or Bel (Lord). Here he set up forms of politics, morals, and economics which were destined to spread throughout the world and to persist even to the present day. Here he established that rebel and evil system which is known in the Bible by the generic term, "Babylon."

The Purposes of God

Once again Satan led the world into darkness and degradation; once again man worshipped the Prince of this World under various guises, and lost all knowledge of his Creator. But once again the Bible shows us the love of God working out His purposes in the affairs of men, and developing His Great Plan of Salvation.

In pursuance of this plan, God, in the person of the Only-begotten Son, was in due time to step down from the throne of the Majesty on high and clothe Himself in human flesh.

So tremendous an event could not be left to mere chance. It was necessary to ensure that, when the time came, there should be a virgin who was fitted in every way to be the mother of so wonderful a child. This mother would, of necessity, belong to some family, and that family to some nation.

Abram and Sarai

For this purpose God did not choose any of the nations which then existed; He chose one man and one woman, Abram and Sarai, and from them created a nation.

Abram's genealogy, which is given in Genesis xi, shows that he was descended from Shem, Noah's son, through Eber, Noah's great-great-grandson, and was, therefore,

26

not only a Semite, but also a Hebrew, as he is described in Genesis xiv, 13.

Sarai, his wife, was also of the same line, being, in fact, a daughter of Abram's father, Terah, by another wife.

Read Genesis xx, 11-12.

These two famous persons were born in the tenth generation from Noah; and it is interesting to note that all their ancestors on the male side, back to Noah himself, lived to see them grow up to maturity.

The Call

To Abram came the command of the Lord, "Get thee out of thy country, and from thy kindred, and from thy father's house, unto a land that I will shew thee."

So great was Abram's faith that he left his native city, Ur of the Chaldees, for a country of which he did not even know the name. As the Epistle to the Hebrews puts it: "By faith Abraham, when he was called to go out into a place which he should after receive for an inheritance, obeyed; and he went out, not knowing whither he went."

Although themselves idolaters, Abram and Sarai believed all the words of the Lord; for with the command came a promise which explained the purpose of their call, the reason for their separation, and the object of their journey: "I will make of thee a great nation, and I will bless thee and make thy name great; and thou shalt be a blessing: and I will bless them that bless thee, and curse him that curseth thee; and in thee shall all families of the earth be blessed."

Read Joshua xxiv, 2; Genesis xi, 27—xii, 5; Hebrews xi, 8.

When Abram and Sarai had obeyed the command of the Lord to the letter; when they had cut themselves off from their country, their clan, and even from their kith and kin; when they had buried Terah at Haran, and parted company with Lot, the Lord repeated His promise.

Read Genesis xiii, 14-17.

The Oath

Meanwhile, the child of promise had not yet been born, and Abram enquired of the Lord. In answer to his prayer,

27

God confirmed the promise and ratified it by a solemn covenant under oath according to the custom of the time.

Read Genesis xv.

The tremendous importance to all mankind of the promise and the oath is heavily stressed in the Epistle to the Hebrews.

Read Hebrews vi, 11-20.

Ishmael

After this Abram had a son by Hagar the Egyptian, and called his name Ishmael. But Ishmael was not destined to be the inheritor of the covenant; the heir must be born of Sarai, and she was barren.

The Child of Promise Delayed

Time passed by, and still the child of promise had not been born. Sarai reached the age of 90, and Abram the age of 99, when both were as good as dead so far as the procreation of children was concerned.

There was, of course, a purpose behind this delay. It must be remembered that Abram, although he was the tenth in the direct line from Noah, through Shem, was nevertheless a product of the corrupt civilization of his time, having been, up to the age of 75, a worshipper of false gods.

It would seem, therefore, that it was necessary to purge the blood of both the chosen founders of the new nation from all those evil influences which they might have inherited or acquired.

The first step in this process was the complete separation of Abram and Sarai from their surroundings, and even from their closest relations.

The next step was the withholding of a child until the natural functions of both had ceased to exist.

Abraham and Sarah

At this advanced age God appeared again to Abram and Sarai and changed their names: Abram (high father) to Abraham (father of a great multitude) and Sarai (my princess) to Sarah (the princess).

Isaac, the Miracle Child

This significant change of names was accompanied by a renewal of the covenant, and a promise that, within a twelvemonth Sarah should be delivered of a son.

The announcement proved too much for the faith of Abraham and Sarah, and they both laughed at the apparent impossibility.

Abraham actually went so far as to plead that Ishmael might be recognised as the heir of the covenant. God's answer that He had already blessed the lad in a different way (as indicated in Genesis xvi, 7-12; xvii, 20; xxi, 12-13 and xxi, 17-18) is of great importance in view of the claim of the Arabs to be descended from Ishmael.

This lapse of faith was rebuked with the words: "Is anything too hard for the Lord?"; and, indeed, it was only momentary as we learn from the New Testament.

Read Genesis xvii, 1-22; xviii, 1-19; Romans iv, 18-22;
Hebrews xi, 11-12.

Within a year from that time the miracle-child was born. After all the long years of waiting the faith of Abraham and Sarah had been justified; their hopes had been fulfilled, and their prayers had been answered. To them had been vouchsafed the son who should be the inheritor, not only of Abraham's great wealth, but also of the glorious destiny of the covenant.

Read Genesis xxi, 1-8.

The Test of Abraham's Faith

To this child Abraham gave the name of Isaac, which means "laughter." Sarah's laughter at his birth was the laughter of joy; but Abraham was obeying the command of the Lord. He had not forgotten that the child had been named "Isaac" before he had even been conceived, as a reminder that both his parents had doubted the intention, and even the power, of God to keep His promise.

Possibly because of this doubt their faith was to be subjected to a further test, and one of even greater severity. For when Isaac had reached the very threshold of manhood, Abraham was commanded to take him to the mountain

29

Moriah, and there to offer him up as a sacrifice to his Creator.

Read Genesis xxii, 1-14.

The sacrifice of a child, even of a favourite child, was no uncommon feature of the heathen religions of the time. The practice is often mentioned in the Old Testament in general terms; while a definite example is recorded as having taken place in the time of Elisha the prophet.

Read 2 Kings iii, 26-27.

In Abraham's case, as we learn from the text, God never intended that the horrible rite should be completed. He used it merely as a trial of faith, and Abraham's triumphant emergence from it is one of the great themes of the Bible.

Read Hebrews xi, 17-19.

The Covenant Unconditional

After this supreme test the covenant is repeated for the seventh time; and it should be noted that no conditions whatever are imposed.

The words of the Lord are not "*If* thou *wilt* obey My voice," but "*Because* thou *hast* done this thing," and "*Because* thou *hast* obeyed My voice."

Read Genesis xxii, 15-18.

Rebekah

Isaac's marriage was a matter of some concern to his father and mother, because it was important that the purity of the Hebrew strain should be preserved in the chosen seed of the covenant line. For this reason an alliance with a Canaanite girl was out of the question; the bride must be sought from among his own kith and kin.

Thus we find Abraham sending his head servant on a long journey northward into Syria, to the region of Padan-aram, to bring back a Hebrew wife for his son.

The story of this strange wooing-by-proxy of Rebekah, Abraham's great-niece, forms a romantic narrative, which may be read in the twenty-fourth chapter of Genesis.

Isaac was forty years old when he married Rebekah; and again it is interesting to note that both Eber and Shem were still alive.

30

The Sons of Keturah

After the death of Sarah, Abraham took another wife, Keturah, by whom he had six sons. These sons were, of course, the seed of Abraham; but, like Ishmael, they were not the chosen seed through whom all the nations of the earth were to be blessed. The Lord's fiat had gone forth: "In Isaac shall thy seed be called."

Read Genesis xxi, 12; Romans ix, 7-9.

The Covenant Confirmed to Isaac

To Isaac, then, as the chosen heir, the Lord confirmed the covenant on two separate occasions: first at Gerar and then at Beer-sheba.

Read Genesis xxvi, 1-5; xxvi, 23-24.

CHAPTER VI

ISRAEL

Esau and Jacob

The next great event after the death of Abraham was the birth to Isaac and Rebekah of twin sons, Esau and Jacob, each one the founder of a nation.

Jacob gained his name, which means "supplanter," from the fact that he took hold of, or tripped up, his elder brother's heel. By taking a mean advantage of him, he fully justified his name; but it must be remembered that this was only possible because Esau despised his birthright.

From the incident of the "red pottage" and also from his appearance, Esau gained for himself the nickname of Edom, which means "red"; in this way he became the progenitor of the Edomites, who were called Idumæans in later times.

Read Genesis xxv, 19-34; xxxvi, 8-9.

Jacob's Double Treachery

Although Esau had sold the birthright of the covenant, he was still the elder son, and therefore the prospective heir of his father's personal property. But of this also Jacob cheated him, with his mother's connivance.

Jacob's Flight

For this act of treachery Esau vowed that he would kill Jacob after his father's death; and it became evident that, if bloodshed was to be avoided, Jacob would have to leave his home.

Moreover, Esau had deeply grieved his father and mother by marrying two Hittite women; and both Isaac and Rebekah were anxious that Jacob should not follow his example.

Thus it came about that Jacob was sent off in some haste to Padan-aram, with instructions to seek out Rebekah's brother, Laban, and to marry one of his daughters.

Read Genesis xxvi, 34—xxviii, 5.

Jacob's Vision

On the way to Padan-aram the Lord appeared to Jacob in a dream, and made him the inheritor of the covenant which he had so greatly coveted, and which Esau had so foolishly despised.

Read Genesis xxviii, 10-15.

The Stone

In the morning the sense of the presence of God was so strong that Jacob named the place Beth-el (House of God). Overcome with awe, he took the stone which he had used for a pillow, set it up as a pillar of witness, and solemnly consecrated it by pouring oil upon it.

Read Genesis xxviii, 16-22.

Rachel

Arrived in Padan-aram, Jacob fell in love with his cousin Rachel, and contracted to serve her father, Laban, seven years for her.

When the seven years had been served, he began to learn that sharp practice was a very unpleasant weapon, especially when that weapon happened to be wielded by another man. For Laban substituted Rachel's elder sister, Leah, and only allowed Jacob to marry Rachel when he had contracted to serve another seven years.

Read Genesis xxix, 1-30.

Jacob's Servitude

At the end of these fourteen years Jacob contracted to serve yet another six years for a certain portion of his uncle's flocks and herds, and again Laban endeavoured to defraud him.

Nor was this all; for during these twenty years Jacob's wages were changed ten times, each time presumably for the worse.

Read Genesis xxxi, 36-42.

Jacob's Conversion

When, at the Lord's command, Jacob broke away from his uncle and set out for his own country with his wives and children, his servants, and the flocks and herds which he had acquired, he was a changed man.

Twenty years of the severest discipline under the unscrupulous Laban had refined his character, and taught him many valuable lessons. But his conversion was not yet complete; he had still to abase himself before his brother, to put his life in his hands, and to make amends for his former treachery.

This was the hardest lesson of all. He was unwilling to admit that he had been in the wrong; his whole being recoiled at the sacrifice of his pride, his possessions, and even, possibly, of his very life.

In due course, however, he arrived at the ford of the brook Jabbok. Here news came to him that Esau was on his way to meet him with four hundred men; and he realised that the dreaded meeting could no longer be avoided.

Israel

This was the great spiritual crisis in Jacob's life, and his surrender to the will of God was complete. The new phase, upon which he now entered, was marked by the divine command that his name, which meant "supplanter," should

c

33

be superseded by the title "Israel," which means "ruling with God."

Read Genesis xxxii, 24-30.

After his reconciliation with Esau, Israel settled down at Shechem. But here the command of the Lord came to him to return to Beth-el, the place of his dream and of the consecrated stone. Accordingly Israel went to Beth-el, and there the covenant was repeated to him for the second time.

When he had again consecrated the stone of witness, Israel set out for Hebron, the home of his father Isaac and of his grandfather Abraham. But on the way Rachel, his favourite wife, died in giving birth to her second son Benjamin, and was buried at Bethlehem.

Read Genesis xxxv, 1-20.

The Children of Israel

Israel had now acquired a family of twelve sons and one daughter by his two wives and their handmaids.

As these twelve sons became the founders of the tribes which afterwards formed the nation of Israel, and as the greater part of the Bible is the history of that nation, it is important that we should note the order of their birth and the names of their mothers.

Son	Mother
(1) Reuben	Leah
(2) Simeon	,,
(3) Levi	,,
(4) Judah	,,
(5) Dan	Bilhah (Rachel's handmaid)
(6) Naphtali	,, ,, ,,
(7) Gad	Zilpah (Leah's handmaid)
(8) Asher	,, ,, ,,
(9) Issachar	Leah
(10) Zebulun	,,
(11) Joseph	Rachel
(12) Benjamin	,,

Read Genesis xxxv, 21-29.

Joseph

It was not unnatural, perhaps, that Joseph should have been his father's favourite child, for he was the elder son of Rachel, Israel's favourite wife.

This preference, however, excited such intense jealousy in the hearts of his brothers that they stopped a camel caravan on its way to Egypt and sold him, at the suggestion of Judah, for twenty pieces of silver. Having thus got rid of him, they told Israel that he was dead.

Read Genesis xxxvii.

Joseph's subsequent adventures in Egypt, and his phenomenal rise to the position of Ruler of all Egypt under the Pharaoh of the time, may be read in Genesis, chapters xxxix-xli.

Israel Goes Down to Egypt

Some seven years later the Near East was visited by one of the severest famines which it has ever known. This lasted for seven whole years, and in the second year Israel and his descendants came to the very verge of starvation.

Meanwhile Joseph, forewarned of God, had stored up large quantities of food for the people of Egypt; and Israel, hearing that food could be bought, sent some of his sons down to Egypt. To their surprise and consternation these men found the brother whom they had sold into slavery occupying a position of immense power.

Remembering their harsh treatment of him, the brothers expected little mercy; but Joseph showed no resentment. Not only did he give them food in abundance, but he also sent wagons to bring his aged father, his brothers, his brothers' wives and their children down to Egypt.

Under the protection of Joseph, and of a well-disposed Pharaoh, this little colony of seventy souls settled in the fertile delta of the Nile, which was then called the Land of Goshen.

The whole of this fascinating story may be read in Genesis, chapters xlii-xlvii.

Israel's Last Words

Seventeen years after his journey to Egypt, Israel died at

the age of 147; but in his last hours he was inspired by the Holy Spirit to utter some remarkable prophecies.

Joseph Chosen

First of all he called Joseph and his two sons to his bedside. To them he announced that he had adopted Manasseh and Ephraim as his own sons, thus making Joseph the founder of two tribes, and the chief inheritor of the covenant.

Ephraim Chosen

His next action was even more surprising and unexpected; for when Joseph led up his two sons to be blessed, Manasseh on his left and Ephraim on his right, Israel deliberately crossed his arms so that his right hand rested on the head of Ephraim, the younger son, and his left hand on the head of Manasseh, the elder.

Thus the major covenant responsibility of becoming "a nation and a company of nations" was conferred upon Ephraim, while the minor responsibility of becoming "a great people" was conferred upon Manasseh.

Read Genesis xlviii.

Prophecies Concerning the Last Days

After this Israel called all his sons together to give them his final blessing, and to reveal what should befall their descendants "in the last days."

As our appreciation of the full scope of Israel's inspired prophecy depends upon a clear understanding of the term "the last days," and as we shall encounter this expression in sundry forms throughout the Bible, we may profitably spend a few moments in considering what it really means.

In ancient times there was, of course, no world-wide system of chronology such as we have to-day. The modern calendar dates backward and forward from the birth of the Christ, so that practically the whole world acknowledges, consciously or unconsciously, that tremendous fact of history.

Similarly, the birth of the Christ divides the "times" of the Bible. In the New Testament we find the B.C. era described as "the former times" or "former days"; while in the Old Testament we find the A.D. era described as "the latter times," "the latter days," "the last times," or "the last days."

The Epistle to the Hebrews contrasts these two periods in a very striking manner, and makes a sharp distinction between the "time past," when God revealed Himself to the Fathers by the Prophets, and "these last days," in which He further reveals Himself to the world by His Son.

Israel's death-bed prophecies, therefore, look forward not only to the First Coming of God the Son as the Anointed Priest, but beyond that to His Second Coming as the Anointed King.

The Birthright

While making these prophecies, Israel settled, once and for all, the question of the inheritance of the Birthright.

This right of primogeniture, or right of the first-born, carried with it many privileges, of which the following are the most important:

(1) The eldest son was consecrated to the Lord.

Read Exodus xxii, 29.

(2) He inherited a double portion of his father's estate.

Read Deuteronomy xxi, 15-17.

(3) He had authority over his brothers and sisters.

Read Genesis xxvii, 29.

(4) He succeeded to the government of his family, tribe, or kingdom.

Read 2 Chronicles xxi, 1-3.

In making his last Will and Testament, Israel passed the covenant on to his sons. But, acting on divine inspiration, he did not bequeath the birthright to Reuben, or to Judah or, indeed, to any of his elder sons. On the contrary, he bequeathed it to Joseph, in trust for Ephraim.

The Stone of Israel

This fact invests the latter part of Genesis xlix, 24 with especial significance. For if the general sense of that sentence is "henceforth he is the shepherd of the stone of Israel," then it would appear that Israel made Joseph the guardian of the stone which he had twice consecrated at Beth-el. Indeed, it is difficult to believe that the passage can bear any other construction; for this sacred stone, by its mute witness to the promises of God, had become, as it were, the title-deed to the covenant.

Judah, the Royal Tribe

Thus all the responsibilities of the birthright were bequeathed to Joseph, with one very important exception. Judah had been passed over, together with all the elder sons; but to him was granted the privilege of founding the tribe from which the promised line of kings should be chosen, and therefore the tribe into which the Messiah should be born.

Read Genesis xlix; Deuteronomy xxxiii, 13-17; 1 Chronicles v, 1-2.

CHAPTER VII

THE ABRAHAMIC COVENANT

It would hardly be possible to exaggerate the importance of the Abrahamic covenant; for it overshadows the whole Bible from the twelfth chapter of Genesis, and all the remaining covenants spring directly from it.

This, the fourth of the eight great covenants of the Bible, contains the promise of the One Seed of Abraham; that is to say, the Greatest Seed, and therefore the greatest blessing to all the families of the earth; and it outlines, in prophecy, God's Great Plan of Salvation from the call of Abraham to the end of the Millennium.

We may, therefore, with profit, spend a few moments in examining the terms of this remarkable charter.

The Responsibility

Before all else the covenant imposed upon Abraham, his son Isaac, his grandson Israel, and upon all the descendants of Israel throughout their generations, the tremendous responsibility of so conducting themselves, in accordance with the will of God, that they might be a blessing to all the families of the earth.

In other words, they were chosen to be a living instrument in the hand of God, a servant nation eager and willing to proclaim God's Great Plan of Salvation to all mankind.

The Privileges

For the discharge of this responsibility they were promised the necessary equipment.

(1) They were to become a great nation.

(2) They were to inherit the land from the River of Egypt to the River Euphrates.

(3) They were to have a dynasty of kings.

(4) They were to spread abroad from Palestine to the west, the east, the north, and the south.

(5) They were to increase in numbers until they could be compared with the dust of the earth, the sand of the sea, and the stars of heaven for multitude.

(6) They were to develop into an empire of an unusual kind, consisting of a mother nation and a commonwealth of independent daughter nations.

(7) They were to possess the gate of their enemies; which may be interpreted as meaning that they were to hold the main strategic points on the face of the earth.

These privileges were bestowed upon the descendants of Abraham, through Isaac and Israel, for one purpose: that by example and precept, but chiefly by example, they might bring the whole world back to the knowledge and love of God.

The Promise and the Oath

In varying terms the covenant was announced seven times to Abraham, twice to Isaac, and three times to Israel, twelve times in all. On the fourth occasion the announcement was confirmed by God with an oath.

The Epistle to the Hebrews states that the promise was confirmed by an oath, because God wished to make it clear beyond all doubt that the terms of the covenant would

39

never be subject to any kind of alteration; and it goes on to show that the promise and the oath, being "two immutable things in which it was impossible for God to lie," must be regarded as an essential and unchangeable part of the counsel of God.

St. Paul informs us that the Messiah came to "confirm the promises made unto the fathers"; while Zacharias refers to the birth of Jesus as a direct fulfilment of the promise and the oath of the Abrahamic covenant.

Read Hebrews vi, 11-20; Romans xv, 8-9; Luke i, 67-75.

The Faithfulness of God

It must be obvious, then, that there is no escape for the honest Christian from the implications of this covenant. Either God made the promises and confirmed them with an oath, or He did not.

If we say that God did not make these promises, then we deny the truth of the Old Testament; and in so doing we deny the teaching of the Lord Jesus, who upheld the Scriptures of His day as the written word of God.

If we say that He did make these promises, but that He has not fulfilled them or will not fulfil them, then we deny the truth of the New Testament, and brand God as a perjurer and a liar.

If we say that God has broken any promise which He has ever made, how can we be certain that He will keep His promise to those who believe in His Son?

CHAPTER VIII

THE PEOPLE

Israel under the Hyksos

When the family of Israel migrated to Egypt, that country was held in subjection by a people called the Hyksos, much in the same way as Britain was once held in subjection by the Romans. These people, if we may accept the evidence of archæologists, were not only Semites, but Hebrews, and therefore of the same stock as the Israelites to whom they were kindly disposed.

Eventually, however, the ancient native dynasty, which had retreated southward up the Nile, returned in great force and drove the Hyksos out of the country. This change of dynasty is described in the Bible by the words: "Now there arose up a new king over Egypt which knew not Joseph."

The Oppression

This new Pharaoh, finding a large and powerful body of aliens akin to the Hyksos, settled in the fertile delta of the Nile, and fearing them as a possible menace to his own security, proceeded to reduce them to a condition of bondage by measures of the severest kind.

Read Exodus i, 1-14.

The Israelites were not driven out of Egypt with the Hyksos because the Egyptians hoped, at one and the same time, to profit by their labour and to prevent their expansion. This policy, astute though it may have been, was only partially successful; for enforced labour, while it prevented effective organisation, in no wise retarded their growth.

Harsher conditions, applied from time to time, failed to solve the problem. The Egyptians were loath to dispense with their slaves, but the Hebrews continued to increase in numbers; moreover, they held the gate of Egypt, and could open it to a foreign power at any time.

Thus we find the Pharaoh of the latter part of Exodus i reduced to the expedient of issuing secret orders to the midwives to murder every Hebrew baby when it happened to be of the male sex.

Read Exodus i, 15-22.

Moses

God, we are told, can bring good out of evil, and make even the wrath of man to turn to His praise; and here surely was a case where He made even the fierceness of this inhuman king redound to His glory. For, as a direct result of Pharaoh's savage order to the midwives, Moses, the future leader of the Israelites, was taken into the royal palace and educated in all the vast knowledge of Egypt.

Read Romans ix, 17; Exodus ii, 1-10; Acts vii, 17-22.

Stephen, the first Christian martyr, tells us that Moses was forty years old when he incurred the displeasure of the reigning Pharaoh and fled to Midian, where he remained for forty years.

In the land of Midian, which lies near the Gulf of Akaba, Moses became the headman of his father-in-law Jethro; and it is reasonable to suppose that, in the course of his duties, he gained first-hand acquaintance with the route over which he afterwards led his fellow-countrymen.

The Call of Moses

On one expedition with his flocks and herds, near Mount Sinai, the angel of the Lord appeared to Moses in a bush which burned with fire, but was not consumed. At the same time the voice of God commanded him to return to Egypt and lead His people out of their bondage into the Promised Land.

No wonder Moses quailed at the magnitude of the task.

In the first place, he had to convince a huge mob of slaves that he was a leader sent from God; he had to encourage these cowed and dispirited men to defy their masters; he had to persuade them to leave their homes and to follow him out into the wilderness.

In the second place, he had to confront the most powerful

42

tyrant in the world and command him to release the slaves who were bringing him so much wealth.

Read Exodus ii, 11—iv, 23; Acts vii, 23-35.

The Deliverance

When he had convinced the Israelites of his mission Moses took his brother Aaron with him, and repeated the words of the Lord to Pharaoh. That monarch, in all the pride of his newly-acquired power, not only refused to let the people go, but made the conditions of their labour even harsher than they had been before.

The hour of the great deliverance had come. God had not forgotten His covenant with Abraham, Isaac and Israel; and He was now about to demonstrate His presence and His power to Hebrew and Egyptian alike.

Read Exodus iv, 27—vi, 13; Genesis xv, 13-14.

The Plagues

Ten terrible plagues had to be visited upon the Egyptians before they would consent to free their slaves, and from all these disasters the Israelites were miraculously protected.

The full account may be read in Exodus, chapters vii-xi. Here we must content ourselves with a summary.

THE TEN PLAGUES OF EGYPT

(1) Water turned into blood.
(2) Frogs.
(3) Lice.
(4) Flies.
(5) Murrain.
(6) Boils and blains.
(7) Hail.
(8) Locusts.
(9) Darkness.
(10) Death of the first-born.

The Passover

The last plague, the death of the first-born of man and beast, was the most terrible scourge of all, and was only visited upon the Egyptians after they had rejected ten distinct opportunities to obey the will of God.

From this plague also the Israelites were wholly protected. Each family received a command to kill a male lamb, free from spot or blemish, and to sprinkle its blood upon the framework of their doorways; and each family received a promise that the Lord would "pass over" any house which was distinguished in this way.

The lamb was to be roasted whole and eaten with unleavened bread and bitter herbs, after they had dressed and equipped themselves for their journey.

Thus was instituted the great festival of the Lord's Passover; for the elaborate ritual which was then laid down was established as a memorial, a feast, and an ordinance for ever by the word of the Lord.

The Paschal Lamb

Later in our studies we shall see that the Paschal Lamb was symbolical of the Messiah, who came to this earth to sacrifice Himself as the spotless "Lamb of God, which taketh away the sin of the world."

He, too, was sacrificed at the Feast of the Passover; and, just as the blood of the paschal lamb sprinkled upon the lintel and sideposts preserved the Israelites from the sword of the angel of death, so the blood of the Lamb of God sprinkled upon the hearts of His followers preserves their bodies and souls unto everlasting life.

Read Exodus xii, 1-36; John i, 29; Corinthians v, 7-8; Revelation v, 6; v, 11-13; xii, 10-11.

The Exodus

Four hundred and thirty years before these great events the patriarch Israel had led down to Egypt a family of seventy souls; when his descendants left the country they must have numbered at least 2,000,000.

From the record we learn that there were "about 600,000 men beside children." One year later there were 603,550 men "from 20 years old and upward," among whom the whole tribe of Levi was not included. If, then, we make an

44

allowance of only one woman and one child to every man, we arrive at the very conservative estimate of 1,800,000.

Read Exodus xii, 37-42; Numbers i, 45-47.

In ordinary circumstances the Exodus would have been a crazy undertaking. This great mass of people, with all their flocks and herds, left Egypt with very scanty provisions, little organisation, and the poorest of military equipment. They were woefully deficient in initiative, in discipline, and in the arts of warfare; while, to make matters worse, their route lay through arid and sterile country.

Humanly speaking, they were bound to perish from hunger, thirst, and the attacks of predatory enemies. Only a miracle or a succession of miracles could have saved them from utter destruction.

In actual fact only a succession of miracles did save them; for God held back the waters of the Red Sea until they had passed through, and loosed them on the pursuing Egyptians; He led them with a cloud by day and a pillar of fire by night; He fed them with manna and quails; He drew water for them from the rock; He gave them the victory over the mighty hosts of Amalek.

Never had there been such a deliverance in the history of any people; never had there been such a demonstration of divine majesty and power.

God was working out His Great Plan of Salvation. "For He remembered His holy promise, and Abraham His servant; and He brought forth His People with joy, and His Chosen with gladness; that they might observe His statutes, and keep His laws."

Read Exodus xiii, 17—xvii; Psalm cv.

CHAPTER IX

THE KINGDOM

Sinai

After they had passed through the Red Sea the Israelites travelled slowly southwards until, in the third month of their journey, they came to Mount Sinai, which lies in the promontory between the two horns of the Red Sea.

Although they had gained their freedom and independence, they were still a disorderly mob, without community of purpose, policy or outlook. It was necessary that they should be welded into a nation; and here, in circumstances of awe-inspiring grandeur, the Lord formed them not only into a nation, but into a kingdom, under Himself as King.

The Constitution

This kingdom, composed as it was of State, Church and divine King, formed a polity without parallel in all history. While the whole nation formed the State, the whole nation also formed the Church, and over both reigned God, supreme Head of both Church and State.

Thus there came into being at Sinai a kingdom, created by God, established by God, and ruled by God; in other words, the one man Abraham had been developed into the Kingdom of God, which was to be the basis, or nucleus, of the universal Kingdom of God over all the earth.

The Giving of the Law

Nor was this the end of the marvels of Sinai; for with her constitution as the Kingdom of God, Israel received the Law of that kingdom direct from God Himself.

Although the Law of the Lord occupies so large a portion of the Bible, it is probably more neglected and more mis-understood than any other part of the great Book; and this may be due in some measure to ignorance of what really happened at Sinai.

The Ascents of Moses

From a careful examination of the text we find that Moses ascended into the mount at least seven times, and each time he received a commission from the Lord, which he placed before the congregation of Israel.

First Ascent

God gave to Moses the constitution of the kingdom, and presented Himself to the people of Israel as their God and King.

Read Exodus xix, 1-7.

Second Ascent

God announced that He would come down upon the mountain in three days' time so that all Israel might hear when He spoke to Moses. At the same time He gave specific instructions for the preparations which were to be made in the interval.

Read Exodus xix, 8-15.

Third Ascent

All Israel was filled with the realisation of the majesty and power of God.

First of all came thunders and lightnings; next a dense cloud; then the shock of a great earthquake, accompanied by fire and smoke; after these the sound of the trumpet of God, filling the air with its insistent challenge; last of all, the voice of God Himself uttering the synopsis of the divine Law, commonly known as the Ten Commandments.

The people were terrified, even Moses being shaken to the very depths of his inmost soul.

Read Exodus xix, 16—xx, 20; Hebrews xii, 18-21.

This great event, the overwhelming grandeur of which baffles the imagination, is sometimes represented as a demonstration of the wrath of God, as in the well-known hymn:

"When God of old came down from heaven,
    In power and wrath He came."

Such a view cannot be too strongly deprecated; for God,

so far from visiting his displeasure on Israel, was conferring upon her the highest honour which He could confer upon any nation.

A truer impression of the glorious message of Sinai may be gained from another famous hymn:

> "O come, O come, Thou Lord of Might,
> Who to Thy tribes, on Sinai's height,
> In ancient times didst give the Law
> In cloud, and majesty, and awe;
> Rejoice! Rejoice! Emmanuel
> Shall come to thee, O Israel."

Fourth Ascent

Moses received the next portion of the Law, which occupies three whole chapters (Exodus xxi-xxiii), and after coming down wrote all the words of the Lord.

Read Exodus xx, 21; xxiv, 3-4.

Fifth Ascent

Moses received a further portion of the Law, which occupies seven more chapters (Exodus xxv-xxxi); and, after forty days' absence, brought down with him two tables of stone written upon by the finger of God.

Read Exodus xxiv, 12-18; xxxi, 18.

Upon reaching the camp, however, Moses found the people indulging in an obscene heathen orgy and worshipping a calf made of molten gold. In his anger he broke the two tablets of stone, ground the golden calf to powder, and executed summary judgment upon the ringleaders.

Read Exodus xxxii, 19-29.

Sixth Ascent

Moses interceded for the people.

Read Exodus xxxii, 30-35.

Seventh Ascent

Moses received yet another portion of the Law, which he was commanded to write, and which occupies six more chapters (Exodus xxxv-xl). Again, when he came down, he brought with him two tables of stone written with the finger of God.

Once more he had been alone with God for forty days and forty nights; and the reflected glory of the Almighty was so strong upon him that the people were afraid to approach him until he had covered his face with a veil.

Read Exodus xxxiv, 1-8; xxxiv, 27-35; Deuteronomy x, 1-5; Exodus xl, 34-38.

Further Portions of the Law

With the last chapter of Exodus we come to the end of the delivery of the Law from Mount Sinai, but further portions of the Law were given to Moses from time to time.

These additions form a large proportion of the books of Leviticus, Numbers, and Deuteronomy. Each is preceeded by the words, "And the Lord spake unto Moses saying," or similar words; and we are told that God spoke to Moses as a man speaks to his friend.

Read Exodus xxxiii, 9-11.

CHAPTER X

THE LAW OF THE LORD

When God created the universe He laid down certain laws for the regulation and control of all those things which He had made; and these laws, being an expression of His very nature, were fixed, unalterable, and everlasting.

Some people prefer to call the laws of God for His Creation, the laws of nature. But whether they be called the laws of nature or the laws of God, their existence has to be recognised and respected. Defiance of the law of gravity, for instance, must inevitably result in serious consequences.

Not only are these laws respected, they are also freely utilised, even when the manner of their operation is not fully understood; as, for example, in agriculture or the employment of electricity.

Thus, while man must recognise, and may make use of,

D
49

the laws of his Creator, he is powerless to interfere with their action. But at the same time he has free will to choose whether he will obey those laws to his own advantage, or disobey them to his hurt.

The Necessity for the Law

During the period between the fall of Adam and the call of Abraham, man gradually lost the power of direct communion with God through his own persistent disobedience, and it became necessary that he should be instructed in that portion of the laws of God which particularly concerned himself.

For this reason the Kingdom of God was created, and the Law of the Lord concerning man was revealed by God to Israel through the mouth of Moses.

The Mosaic Law

It is unfortunate, perhaps, that the Law of the Lord should have become so generally known as the Mosaic Law, because that description may possibly convey the impression that the Law of Israel was compiled by Moses, much in the same way as the laws of Athens were compiled by Solon, or the laws of Sparta by Lycurgus.

Such an impression would be utterly at variance with the teaching of the Bible, for nothing could be clearer than the fact that the Law was not the product of the brain of any man, but the expression of the unalterable will of the Creator.

Jesus the Law-giver

From the New Testament we learn that the creation of the universe was the especial work of God the Son. "All things were made by Him; and without Him was not anything made that was made." The Law of the Lord was therefore the expression of the unalterable will of God the Son.

Read John i, 1-3; Hebrews i, 1-2; i, 8-10.

Did God the Son, when He came to this world in human flesh, revoke the Law which He had Himself revealed at Mount Sinai?

There can be only one answer. Nevertheless, it is con-

50

stantly asserted, with complete disregard of logic, that the Law of the Lord, as entrusted to Israel, is not binding upon any nation, kingdom, people, or individual to-day.

It is, indeed, one of the strangest of paradoxes that men and women who call themselves Christians should deny, and even ridicule, the words of the Master whom they profess to serve. For our Lord's own declaration concerning the Law is expressed in terms which exclude any possible misunderstanding.

Read Matthew v, 17-19; Luke xvi, 17.

Three Divisions of the Law

The Sinaitic code falls naturally into three main divisions, which are called in the Bible the statutes, the judgments, and the ordinances. These divisions may be described in general terms as follows.

The Statutes

Laws concerning every phase of human activity, religious, moral, social, economic, political, and international.

The Judgments

Applications of the statutes to particular cases, under divine inspiration; legal precedents.

The Ordinances

Laws relating to the ritual of divine worship, the construction and furnishing of the Tabernacle, the vestments and functions of the Aaronic priesthood, the feasts and fasts, and the various offerings and sacrifices.

The Purpose of the Ordinances

The ritual of the ordinances was designed to accustom the people to a very difficult idea, that of vicarious sacrifice. To this end elaborate ceremonial was laid down for the slaughter of certain animals and birds, as atonement for the sins of the people.

The mere sacrifice of these dumb creatures was, of course, powerless in itself to take away the guilt of sin, and could only be effective by anticipation of the only sacrifice which was really acceptable to the Father.

51

The ordinances, therefore, typified the Messiah, and were intended to prepare Israel for His Coming; or, as St. Paul puts it, they were to be Israel's schoolmaster to bring her to Christ.

The fulfilment of the Law

When God the Son came to this earth in human flesh, He fulfilled—that is to say, He completed and perfected—His own Law by sacrificing Himself on Calvary for the sins of the whole world.

In this supreme act of sacrifice He was, at one and the same time, both the victim sacrificed and the sacrificing priest. As victim He became the last, perfect, all-sufficient sacrifice for sin, the Lamb of God which taketh away the sins of the world.

As priest He became the last great immortal High Priest, and the only Mediator between God and man.

By His life, death, resurrection, and ascension God the Son fulfilled the "end," or purpose, of the ordinances, which then became obsolete by reason of their very fulfilment.

Read Psalm xl, 6-8; Hebrews ix, 24—x, 14; Romans x, 4; Galatians iii, 19-29; Colossians ii, 13-14.

The Statutes Not Superseded

It may be said, therefore, that the Christian religion has superseded the ordinances. But it cannot be said with truth that faith in the Lord Jesus has abolished the statutes; indeed, St. Paul flatly repudiates the very suggestion.

Read Romans iii, 31.

The Law Endorsed by Jesus

The great Apostle's statement leaves no room for misunderstanding; nevertheless, we will turn once more to the highest authority—the Founder of Christianity Himself.

As we do so, let us note one very important fact. In setting an example for all men to follow, our Lord Himself obeyed the Law.

He denounced, in no uncertain terms, the abuses and errors which had crept into it; but His own Law, as revealed to Israel through Moses, He scrupulously obeyed; and throughout His ministry He insisted upon strict obedience to the Law as an essential part of the Christian life.

There are two scenes in the life of Jesus which bring this truth to our notice very forcibly.

The Scene with the Lawyer

In the first scene, Jesus had just answered a question which had been put to Him by the Sadducees, when a lawyer, who was standing in the crowd, asked Him another question: "Which is the greatest commandment of all?"

Read Mark xii, 28-34.

The Scene with the Rich Young Man

In the second scene, a young man ran up to Jesus, knelt down, and blurted out the remarkable question: "Good Master, what shall I do that I may inherit eternal life?"

Read Mark x, 17-22.

The Christian Life

Up to a certain point the two scenes are very much alike. The scribe expressed the greatest reverence for the Law, and Jesus told him that he was "not far from the Kingdom of God"; the rich young ruler said that he had kept the Law from his youth up, "then Jesus, beholding him, loved him." Taken together, these two scenes give us a wonderful outline from the lips of the Lord Himself, of the life of a true Christian. Before all else, obedience to the Law of the Lord, the basic principle of which is love, love of God and love of one's fellow-man; then alms-giving which springs from love; and lastly self-sacrifice and self-surrender, the proofs of love.

The Decalogue

In answering the rich young man, Jesus quoted from the Decalogue, the first ten of all the commandments which He delivered at Sinai. Because He frequently quoted from these ten commandments, and because He often made use of the phrase "the commandments of God," it has been assumed by some careless students that He upheld the Decalogue to the exclusion of the rest of the Law.

The Ten Commandments are, however, a summary, or epitome, of all the commandments of the Law; they are, as it were, the Law in miniature. As we have already noted, in the scene with the lawyer Jesus made an even closer summary of the Law, when He stated that the two great principles which upheld the whole code were love of God and love of one's fellow-man.

Read Matthew xxii, 34-40.

Jesus' Teaching Concerning the Law

Immediately after stating in the most emphatic language that He had not come to destroy the Law, Jesus dealt with six commandments, three of which were taken from the Decalogue, and three from the rest of the Statute Book.

His purpose was not to alter, or correct, the moral principles of the Law, but to refute the false interpretations of the scribes and Pharisees; and so far from destroying, or even weakening the Law, He established it with even greater stringency.

Thus He put anger on the same plane as murder, and the desire for adultery on the same level as adultery itself. He made the law for divorce even more drastic, and tightened up the law regarding the use of oaths. In the case of personal injury, He advocated forgiveness rather than recourse to the strict justice of the Law; and He enjoined love of one's enemies equally with love of one's friends.

Read Matthew v, 17-48.

Our Lord's whole-hearted approbation of the Law and, indeed, of all the Old Testament Scriptures, is one of the salient features of His teaching.

When He alluded, as He frequently did, to "the Law and the Prophets," the Jews, to whom He was speaking, knew perfectly well that He meant the Books of the Law and the Books of the Prophets; and "Moses," in the parlance of the day, was a common abbreviation for the five Books of Moses which contained the Law.

Strange as it may seem, one of the chief causes of the unpopularity of Jesus with the Jewish authorities was His insistence upon strict observance of the Law.

The scribes and the Pharisees sat "in Moses' seat"; that is to say, they administered the Mosaic Law; but they themselves deliberately broke the Law whenever it was profitable to do so. Therefore Jesus warned His disciples not to imitate the corrupt practices of the scribes and Pharisees, but in all things to obey the Law of the Lord.

Read Matthew xxiii, 1-4; John vii, 19.

Not once, but many times, our Lord rebuked the Jews for their contempt of the Old Testament Scriptures; and His words, although spoken to the Jews, are equally true for all time.

In the parable of the Rich Man and Lazarus, Jesus indicated that if the world refuses to read, and to believe, the Books of Moses and the Books of the Prophets, then it will not be persuaded to embrace the Christian faith, even by the fact of His own resurrection from the dead.

In another speech to the Jews He made it clear that belief in the first five books of the Bible will lead to belief in Himself, while disbelief in the books will shake the Christian faith to its very foundations.

Read Luke xvi, 19-31; John v, 39-47.

It is a noteworthy fact that the Lord Jesus, after He had risen from the dead, never withdrew a single statement which He had made during His mortal life.

On the day of His resurrection He appeared to two disciples on the way to Emmaus, and after upbraiding them with their lack of faith in the Books of the Prophets, expounded unto them in all the Scriptures the things concerning Himself, beginning with the Books of Moses.

Read Luke xxiv, 25-27.

Later in the same evening He appeared to the eleven apostles in Jerusalem, and turned the floodlight of His knowledge upon the pages of the Old Testament; He unfolded to them God's Great Plan of Salvation, and His own tremendous part in the fulfilment of it; and He showed them how this was revealed and foretold in the Books of the Prophets, in the Psalms, and in the Mosaic Law.

Read Luke xxiv, 44-48.

The Commandments of Jesus

With these thoughts in our minds we can arrive at a better understanding of our Lord's command to all His followers: "If ye love Me, keep My commandments."

Read John xiv, 15.

God the Son, Creator of the world and Maker of its laws, codified His laws and established them as the Law of the Kingdom which He formed for Himself at Sinai.

When He came to this earth as the Messiah, He fulfilled those portions of the Law which it was necessary for Him to fulfil; and the Law, thus perfected and completed, He endorsed as His commandments.

The failure of Christianity to win the whole world is due to the fact that the commandments of God the Son, codified by Him at Sinai, perfected by Him during His mortal life, have not been kept by the so-called Christian nations.

The infidel points the finger of scorn at our selfishness, our greed, our poverty, our diseases, our quarrels, our wars, and asks what 2,000 years of Christianity have done to relieve the misery of life for the teeming millions of mankind.

The Law of the Lord Jesus offers immunity from all these evils in return for obedience to His commandments.

If civilization to-day finds itself on the brink of an abyss, that is the fault, not of the Founder of Christianity, but of those nations and individuals who have failed to keep the Law of the Lord.

Because of that failure the whole world suffers, and must continue to suffer, until the feet of God the Son stand once more upon the Mount of Olives, and the Law goes forth from Jerusalem to bring order out of chaos, and to establish His reign of righteousness and peace upon the earth.

Read Isaiah ix, 6-7; xlii, 1-4; xxvi, 8-9; Micah iv, 1-5; 1 John ii, 1-7.

CHAPTER XI

THE FORTY YEARS IN THE WILDERNESS

The thunders of Sinai, which reverberate, as it were, throughout the Bible, inaugurate a new era in the fulfilment of the promise to Abraham, Isaac and Israel, and a new phase in the development of God's Great Plan of Salvation.

Israel's descendants have now become a nation; as a nation they have accepted the Lord Jehovah as their king; from their God and King they have received a constitution, a religion, and a code of law; in short, they have become the Kingdom of God on earth.

This great honour brings with it equally great responsibilities, and for these Israel is not as yet prepared; she has much to learn and also much to unlearn.

Brought out of Egypt by the mighty hand and outstretched arm of God, nothing has been required of her as the price of liberty, except patience under certain unavoidable hardships; nevertheless, every step of the journey to Sinai has been marred by open discontent, flaring up at times into rebellion and threats against the life of their great leader.

Accustomed to giving grudging and sullen service only when compelled to do so by their Egyptian taskmasters, the adult generation has failed to rise to the occasion and to shed the mentality of the slave. The adult generation is therefore unfit to enter the Promised Land, and must be allowed to die out; while the younger generation must be educated in the principles of the Law, and trained to obedience by forty years of discipline in the wilderness.

Read Psalm xcv, 7-11.

At the end of this forty years Israel is a strong, virile nation, ready to march in and take possession of Canaan. This, however, is no light undertaking, for the land is held by powerful, warlike tribes, who are ready to dispute every inch of the way. Unaided, the Children of Israel are bound to fail; and Moses warns them that their only hope of success lies in obedience to the Law of the Lord.

Read Deuteronomy viii—x, 7.

God's Judgment on the Canaanites

The campaign in Canaan is to be a war to the death, without truce and without quarter; for by the command of the Lord, the inhabitants of the land are to be exterminated, and their possessions burnt with fire.

Few passages in the Bible have been more grossly misinterpreted than this command; even Christians, it would seem, have been more eager to impute savagery to their Creator than to discover the truth.

Yet the Bible makes it perfectly clear, in the words of God Himself, that the reason for the destruction of the Canaanites was their own appalling iniquity.

It is also clear that God, so far from indulging in an act of fiendish cruelty, only executed judgment upon the Canaanites after more than four centuries had been granted for repentance. Abraham was not allowed to possess the land during his lifetime, and he was told that his descendants would have to reside in a strange land for four hundred years, because, to use the words of the text, "the iniquity of the Amorites is not yet full."

Read Genesis xv, 13-16; Deuteronomy ix, 4-6; xx, 16-18; Leviticus xviii, 19-30.

Canaan was at that time the home of witchcraft and idolatry. Satan was worshipped under the names of various gods and goddesses, in whose religions sexual impurity was exalted into a virtue. Public worship frequently began with human sacrifice, and ended in orgies of indescribable obscenity, with the result that disease raged unchecked throughout the land.

The danger of contamination to a young nation, whose blood had been purified by the severe discipline of the wilderness, may be gathered from the strict regulations which were laid down in the Law, and also from the result of Israel's participation in a feast to Baal-Peor.

Read Leviticus xv; Numbers xxv, 1-9; Deuteronomy iv, 1-9; 1 Corinthians x, 7-8.

So corrupt was the condition of Canaan that it may be compared with the condition of the world before the Flood, and also with that of Sodom and Gomorrah.

For the cleansing of the world before the Flood God used water; for the cleansing of Sodom and Gomorrah He used fire; for the cleansing of the land of Canaan God used the nation which He had formed for Himself, and which, in after days, He called His "battleaxe and weapons of war."

Read Jeremiah li, 19-20.

CHAPTER XII

THE MOSAIC COVENANT

*　　*　　*　　*

Not to be Confused with the Mosaic Law

Although the Mosaic Law and the Mosaic Covenant are so closely interwoven, care must be taken not to confuse the one with the other. The Mosaic Law is a codification of universal law, while the Mosaic Covenant is strictly national and applies to Israel only.

Not a Substitute for the Abrahamic Covenant

It must also be clearly understood that the Mosaic Covenant does not replace the Abrahamic Covenant or, indeed, invalidate it in any way.

The Abrahamic Covenant was, and is still, unbreakable and unconditional, depending solely upon the oath and honour of Almighty God. The Mosaic Covenant, on the other hand, was both breakable and conditional, depending as it did, upon Israel's obedience to the Law.

Read Galatians iii, 15-19.

If and But

The condition of obedience, which is one of the distinguishing features of the Mosaic Covenant, has earned for it the nickname of the "IF AND BUT" Covenant. IF Israel chose to obey the Law, then the Covenant would remain unbroken

59

and certain blessings, or advantages, would follow. BUT if Israel chose to disobey the Law, then the Covenant would be broken, and certain curses, or disadvantages, would be incurred.

The Old Covenant and the New Covenant

In the New Testament the Mosaic Covenant is called the Old Covenant; while in the Old Testament the Covenant in Christ Jesus is called the New Covenant.

Thus we find the Bible divided into two volumes: the Book of the Old Covenant, and the Book of the New Covenant.

The Two Parts of the Mosaic Covenant

So far we have been considering the Mosaic Covenant as a whole. Now we must consider it in its two separate parts: (a) the Covenant made by God with Israel at Sinai; (b) the Covenant made by God with Israel at the River Jordan. These two parts form the Fifth and Sixth Covenants of the Bible.

*   *   *   *

The Fifth Covenant

God's very first words from Sinai set forth the preliminary terms of the Fifth Covenant. As a people, Israel was offered the opportunity of becoming an holy nation, a nation set apart for the service of God. As a nation, Israel was offered the opportunity of becoming God's own peculiar treasure, God's own particular kingdom, the Kingdom of God on earth. As the Kingdom of God, Israel was offered the opportunity of becoming a kingdom of priests, a kingdom of servants to God and ministers to all mankind. Only one condition was imposed: "If ye will obey My voice indeed, and keep My covenant."

These terms were laid by Moses before the elders of the people; and it is significant that the Law was not codified and entrusted to Israel until the broad outlines of the Covenant had been accepted by the representatives of the nation.

Read Exodus xix, 1-8.

60

Shortly afterwards the exact terms of the Covenant were set forth in detail. These terms fall naturally into two divisions, the IF clauses, and the BUT clauses.

The "If" Clauses

The first division enumerates the blessings, or advantages, which Israel would enjoy if she obeyed the Law of the Lord.

Read Leviticus xxvi, 1-13.

The "But" Clauses

The second division describes the curses, or disadvantages, which would fall upon Israel if she rejected the Law of the Lord.

Read Leviticus xxvi, 14-39.

Seven Times

In these clauses God warns the people of His newly-established kingdom that, if they break their part of the Covenant by rejecting the Law, He will punish them "seven times" for their sins.

The significance of the expression "seven times" is not immediately apparent, although its importance is emphasized by a fourfold repetition in the text. We must therefore search elsewhere for a clue to its meaning.

Such a clue we find in the last book of the Bible, where it is revealed to us by our Lord Himself. The twelfth chapter of the Book of Revelation is one in which the Ascended Christ rapidly reviews the early history of the world; in it He describes Satan as the Great Red Dragon, and Israel as the mother of the man-child who will eventually rule all nations with a rod of iron.

Verses 6 and 14 of this chapter describe the same event in different terms. In verse 6 the duration of Israel's "nourishment in the wilderness" is given as "1,260 days," while in verse 14 it is stated as "a time, times, and half a time."

Assuming the minimum number of "times," we reach the conclusion that "$3\frac{1}{2}$ times" equals 1,260 days.

Bearing in mind that a prophetical "day" generally (but not always) indicates an historic year, we reach the further

61

conclusion that "$3\frac{1}{2}$ times" is equivalent to 1,260 historical years.

It is only necessary now to double these figures in order to see that the expression "seven times" betokens a period of 2,520 years.

Thus Israel, having voluntarily entered into a solemn Covenant with God, bound herself to 2,520 years of punishment if she failed to keep her word.

Read Revelation xii, 6 and 14.

The Mercy of God

Even while He was making this Covenant, God knew that Israel would fail to keep it, and would, some seven centuries later, bring upon herself the full curse of the Law.

Yet, knowing all this, God promised that He would not utterly cast His people away, but would remember His Covenant with Abraham, Isaac and Israel, and would be ready, even during this vast period of punishment, to forgive His people when they made national repentance and replaced His Law upon their Statute Book.

In this gracious promise is foreshadowed the redemption of Israel from the curse of the Law by the Messiah, and her ultimate repentance and conversion under the New Covenant in Christ Jesus.

Read Leviticus xxvi, 40-46.

*   *   *   *

The Sixth Covenant

We have already seen that after forty years of training in the wilderness, the Israelites had become sufficiently disciplined to undertake the conquest of the land of Canaan.

Journeying steadily northward they arrived eventually at the eastern bank of the River Jordan, which formed a natural barrier between them and their main objective, the fortified cities on the western side.

Here they encamped; here they prepared for the crossing of the river, and the fighting which must follow; and here God made with them another covenant, the second part of the Mosaic Covenant, and the Sixth Covenant of the Bible.

Read Deuteronomy iv, 1-13; iv, 25-40; xxviii—xxx.

The Choice

In this Covenant the choice between prosperity and want, between health and sickness, between peace and war, between good and evil, between light and darkness, between life and death, between Jehovah and Satan, was placed once more before the Children of Israel.

This has in actual fact been the inevitable choice before every nation, every kingdom, every people, and every individual from the creation of Adam up to the present day. For the Law of the Lord has always been in existence because it was, is, and must ever continue to be, the unchanging expression of the will of God.

Cause and Effect

Of all the natural creation, man alone has received the gifts of free will, which includes the right to decide for himself whether he will, or will not, obey the Law of the Lord.

For man's benefit the Law was codified by God Himself at Sinai; and in the Law the elementary principles of cause and effect were set forth in terms which could be grasped and understood without difficulty by the finite mind of man.

Health, prosperity and peace are the natural consequences of obedience to the Law; while sickness, distress and war wait upon defiance. Effect follows cause as surely as night follows day. Man is as powerless to interfere with the operation of the Law as he is to regulate the revolution of the earth, for both are the expression of the will of the Creator.

The Modern Attitude

The Book of Common Prayer is a national heirloom, the exclusive property of no particular denomination. Those of us who use it make humble confession to Almighty God in the words, "We have offended against Thy Holy Laws."

We make this confession week by week, and even day by day. But too often, alas, we allow the devices and desires of our hearts to lay a smoke-screen between ourselves and the truth, with the consequences that we do not pause to consider what God's Holy Laws really are, and where they may be found.

In our arrogance we exalt our own puny cleverness above the wisdom of the Source of all knowledge; and, in doing so, we draw down upon ourselves the condemnation of God the Son, who is the Way, the Truth and the Life.

"Thus have ye made the commandment of God of none effect by your tradition.

"Ye hypocrites, well did Esaias prophesy of you saying, This people draweth nigh unto Me with their mouth, and honoureth Me with their lips; but their heart is far from Me.

"But in vain do they worship Me, teaching for doctrines the commandments of men."

Read Matthew xv, 6-9.

Consequences of Disbelief

Because the world, for the most part, has rejected the Bible as God's word written, it fails to realise one simple fact: that the terrible scourges of poverty, disease and war are the direct consequence of opposition to the Law which was made for man by his Creator, and which was revealed to man by God Himself at Sinai.

Israel's Responsibility

The Law of the Lord was entrusted to Israel for demonstration to the rest of the world. Indeed, the practical demonstration of the Law was one of the main reasons for the development of Israel as a nation.

Gentile nations were to be invited to study the Law in operation and to observe the benefits which ensued, in order that they might themselves adopt the Law and enjoy the same advantages.

Any failure on the part of Israel to keep the Law would not only bring suffering upon herself, but would cause the Gentile nations to suffer too; and in this way Israel would bring, not a blessing, but a curse upon all the families of the earth.

The magnitude of Israel's responsibility accounts for the severity of the punishment which was to be visited upon her if she disobeyed, as God knew she would. For even while

He was making this Covenant, God revealed to Moses exactly what Israel would do.

Read Deuteronomy xxxi, 16-21.

God would not, and could not, break His unconditional Covenant with Abraham, Isaac and Israel. But He could, and He would, chastise His people with "seven times," or 2,520 years, of His disfavour for breaking the Mosaic Covenant; and this in order that they might, in the "latter times," take up their responsibility anew under the Covenant in Christ Jesus.

CHAPTER XIII

THE CONQUEST OF CANAAN

When the Sixth Covenant was made with the Children of Israel, they were encamped on the eastern bank of the River Jordan, where they were making their final preparations for the invasion of the land of Canaan.

Of all the adult generation which had come out of Egypt none was allowed to take part in this expedition, except Caleb and Joshua. Aaron the High Priest had been buried in Mount Hor; and even Moses, who was still in full possession of all his faculties at the age of 120, was only permitted a distant view of the Promised Land in the hour of his death.

The nomadic days were finished. Israel, under her new leader Joshua, was now to acquire a domicile, and to take her place among the nations of the earth.

Read Joshua v, 6; Deuteronomy xxxiv.

The full details of the conquest of Canaan, the miraculous crossing of the Jordan (which was then in a state of flood), the taking of Jericho, the storming of Ai, and all the other wonders of this campaign, form a fascinating story which may be read in the Book of Joshua.

Archæological Confirmation

In passing, however, we must pay a tribute to those archæologists who have done so much to prove the historical accuracy of the Bible; as, for instance, in their confirmation

of the collapse of the walls of Jericho, and in their discovery
of alphabetical script prior to the time of Moses.

Partition of the Land

At the end of the campaign two tribes and a half had been
established on the eastern side of the Jordan; while the
remaining ten and a half tribes had partitioned the district
on the western side of the Jordan among themselves.

A region approximating in size to that of an English
county was allotted to each tribe, with the exception of the
tribe of Levi, which was a tribe set apart for the service of
the whole community and, as such, only received the revenues
of certain cities.

The Promises to the Fathers

In the settlement of the descendants of Israel upon the
land which had been promised to Abraham, we recognise
yet another process in God's fulfilment of His Covenant
with Abraham, Isaac and Israel.

The Children of Israel have now become a nation, but
not yet a company of nations.

They have entered into possession of the Promised Land,
but not into the whole of it.

They have been developed into a kingdom, with a country,
a king, a constitution, a code of law, and a religion.

The Purpose

Under God's watchful care a powerful nation has been
created from one man; a new kingdom, unique in character,
has taken its place among the kingdoms of the earth.

The Kingdom of God, created by God, developed by God,
trained by God, and ruled by God, has come into being in
pursuance of God's Great Plan of Salvation, and with one
supreme object in view: that the descendants of Abraham,
through Isaac and Israel, may put the Law of the Lord
into practice and demonstrate it to the Gentiles; that, in so
doing, they may become the servants of God, and witnesses
to His truth; that they may prepare the world for the coming
of the Saviour; and that, in all these ways, they may be a
blessing to all the families of the earth.

Read Isaiah xliii, 8-21.

CHAPTER XIV

THE HOUSE OF DAVID

For a period of 334 years, or thereabouts, Israel was ruled directly by God Himself through the agency of judges and prophets. The judges occupied the position of ministers of state, while the prophets were men who received direction from God, and spoke for Him to the nation.

During this period the Children of Israel were by no means the model people which they should have been; for as they came into closer contact with other nations, they began to cast longing eyes upon strange religions and forms of government.

High Treason

Little by little the cults of Baal, Ashtaroth, and other heathen gods and goddesses, with all their hideous, obscene practices, were insinuated into the country; little by little loyalty to the divine King was undermined, until eventually they demanded a king and constitution like those of the nations which lay round about.

This was a very serious breach of the Mosaic Covenant, under which Israel had accepted the Lord Jehovah as her King for all time. Israel had, indeed, violated the main condition of the Covenant, "If ye will obey My voice indeed, ye shall be unto Me a kingdom"; and this perfidy was sufficient to bring upon her the full curse of the Law: banishment from the land, and dispersion among the Gentiles.

Therefore Samuel the prophet prayed to the Lord in fear and trembling, expecting to hear the doom of his country. But that doom was not pronounced. Even Samuel, great prophet as he was, could hardly believe his ears when he heard the gracious reply of the Lord: "Hearken unto their voice, and make them a king."

The Patience of God

We are accustomed to hearing the statement that the God

of the Old Testament was a harsh, cruel, vengeful God, utterly unlike the God of the New Testament, as if there were two Gods in the Bible. But here, as elsewhere, the Lord Jehovah proved the truth of the Psalmist's estimate of His character: "Thou, O Lord, art a God full of compassion and gracious, long-suffering, and plenteous in mercy and truth."

Read Psalm lxxxvi, 15.

God could say to Samuel: "They have not rejected thee, but they have rejected Me, that I should not reign over them," and yet suspend the punishment which Israel deserved, until it could be delayed no longer.

Read 1 Samuel viii.

The Royal Tribe

It will be remembered that this demand for a human king had been foreseen and provided for in the Abrahamic Covenant. The blessing of "kings" had been promised, first to Abraham, then to Sarah, and finally to Israel, who had bequeathed the privilege of providing these kings to his fourth son, Judah.

The First Human King of Israel

Saul, the first king selected by God, was the son of influential parents, a young man of magnificent physique and goodly to look upon. He was a king after the people's own heart, and yet he proved himself just such a tyrant as God had warned them he would be. He was, moreover, not of the royal tribe of Judah, but of the tribe of Benjamin.

From these facts it is evident that Saul was selected with the object of teaching Israel a lesson, and not for the purpose of founding a royal house in accordance with the terms of the Abrahamic Covenant.

Read 1 Samuel ix, 1-2.

David

The great privilege of founding the royal house had been reserved for a scion of the tribe of Judah, by name David, eighth son of Jesse the Bethlehemite.

Many years before the death of Saul, Samuel the prophet

was sent to anoint David as Saul's successor. David at this time was a graceful, well-formed youth on the very threshold of manhood. As the cadet of the family he was taking charge of his father's sheep, and leading a life of quiet contemplation under the open sky, with little company save that of his father's herdsmen. During this period he acquired his skill on the harp, his gift for poetry, and also his great faith in God.

Read 1 Samuel xvi.

Samuel's visit changed the whole course of David's career, and from that time he led a life of adventure such as seldom falls to the lot of any man.

After Saul's death he ascended the throne and in seven and a half years' time had finally consolidated his position as king over all Israel. During his reign he captured Jerusalem and purchased the site on which the Temple was afterwards built; he suppressed idolatry; he restored the Law of the Lord; and as a consequence he raised his kingdom to a very high level of influence and power.

With all his faults he was a generous and lovable character; in Biblical language he was "a man after God's own heart"; and with him God made a Covenant, the Seventh of the Covenants of the Bible, to which we must devote a separate chapter.

Solomon

The reign of Solomon, David's son and successor, may be described as the golden age of Israel's history. He built the Temple which his father had contemplated; the worship of Jehovah was the religion of the land; the Law of the Lord was the law of his kingdom; and the prosperity of his country was the talk of all the bazaars of the East.

CHAPTER XV

THE DAVIDIC COVENANT

In studying the covenants of the Bible it is essential that we should understand, so far as may be, where and how each one fits into God's Great Plan of Salvation.

Each covenant has its own distinctive character and its own distinctive purpose; but all eight covenants blend together in one grand theme, which has for its climax the millennial reign of God the Son.

God's Great Plan came into operation at the very moment when Satan had succeeded in bringing the whole Adamic race under the curse of death. For this murderous act Satan was himself cursed, and the terms of his sentence contain the first disclosure of the divine purpose.

"Because thou hast done this," said the Lord God, "I will put enmity between thee and the woman, and between thy seed and her seed; it shall bruise thy head, and thou shalt bruise his heel." In these words the veil between man and the future was drawn aside just far enough to allow a glimpse of the central figure of the Bible, "the lamb slain from the foundation of the world."

From the seed of the woman was to arise a Deliverer who should "come to seek and to save that which was lost"; a man who should suffer in the fight with Satan, but nevertheless gain the victory; a Saviour who should regain for man that immortal body, "made in the image and likeness of God," which man himself had forfeited.

Thus the age-long struggle between good and evil entered upon a new phase, in the fight between God the Son and Satan for the souls of men.

The Creation of the Kingdom

In pursuance of His Plan God chose one man and one woman to found a nation which should carry out His purposes in the earth; a servant nation which should be ready to receive His Son, and to prepare the world for His Coming.

This man and woman (Abraham and Sarah) He developed into a family, the twelve sons of Israel; that family He developed into a nation, the nation of Israel; and to the nation of Israel He proclaimed Himself King, with the full consent of the people.

Israel's Sin

Thus the Kingdom of God on earth was brought into being. But after nearly 350 years of divine government Israel rejected the Lord Jehovah as her reigning sovereign, and demanded a human king.

This request God granted, knowing full well that the Abrahamic Covenant had been only partially fulfilled. Israel had yet to become a nation and a company of nations or, in other words, an empire; and she had not yet proved herself a blessing to all the families of the earth.

In granting this request it must not be supposed that God abandoned all claim to the kingship of Israel. On the contrary, the throne of Israel still remained the throne of the Lord; the people of Israel still remained God's people; and the kingdom of Israel still remained the Kingdom of God, with a destiny which He has sworn to fulfil.

The Necessity for the Davidic Covenant

In these circumstances it became necessary to ensure the continuity of the kingdom through a line of mortal kings, who should hold the Throne of the Lord in trust until such time as the Abrahamic Covenant had been further fulfilled, and Israel should be willing to restore the kingdom to its rightful Owner.

The Making of the Covenant

Thus it came to pass that God chose David out of the royal tribe of Judah, to found a royal house, or dynasty, over the kingdom of Israel, which should endure for all time.

The announcement of this great favour came to David at a moment of great disappointment. For many years he had cherished the intention of building a permanent house, or temple, for the worship of God, in place of the Taber-

71

nacle; and one day, sitting in the new palace which he had
built in Jerusalem, he made his plans known to Nathan the
prophet.

That same night, however, Nathan was commanded to
tell David that the wish of his heart must be carried out
by Solomon his son. David was not to be allowed to build
a house for the Lord, but the Lord Himself would build a
house for David by making him the founder of an everlasting dynasty.

Read 2 Samuel vii, 1-17.

The Appointed Place

One statement in the Covenant immediately rivets our
attention, if only by its seeming irrelevance. God declared
that He would plant His people in an appointed place,
whence they should move no more, and where they should
be safe from the attacks of their enemies.

As Israel was at that time firmly planted in the Promised
Land, the "appointed place" could not possibly be Palestine.
Moreover, the "planting in an appointed place" implied
an uprooting before Israel could be planted again; and this,
as we shall see, is exactly what happened some 300 years
later.

We realise, then, that this particular statement, so far from
being irrelevant, is an indispensable part of the Davidic
Covenant; for in this promise God, knowing the vicissitudes
through which Israel and the House of David must pass in
the future, makes the revelation that He has already provided
for the continuance of both Kingdom and Throne.

Read Psalm lxxxix, 1-4; 18-37.

Solomon

After David's death the Covenant was confirmed to his
son Solomon.

Read 1 Kings ix, 1-9.

The Throne of the Lord

That David regarded the throne of Israel as the Throne
of the Lord, and himself as nothing more than God's vice-
regent, is evident from his great speech to the solemn

72

assembly of Israel before his abdication in favour of his son Solomon.

Read 1 Chronicles xxviii, 4-5; xxix, 10-11.

In the official record of Solomon's coronation, we again find the throne of Israel described as the Throne of the Lord, and the king as the Lord's Anointed.

Read 1 Chronicles xxix, 22-23.

The Covenant Unconditional

No condition whatsoever is imposed under this Covenant, which depends solely on the honour of God. True, David's successors upon the throne, called in Psalm lxxxix "his children," are to be punished, and punished severely, for any failure to uphold the Law of the Lord; but the royal line is to remain unbroken.

The throne of David is the Throne of the Lord, and it will continue for ever; for in God's good time the last king of the mortal line will hand it back to the Everlasting King, God the Son, who is Himself of the house and lineage of David.

Read Micah v, 2; Luke i, 30-33; Isaiah ix, 6-7.
Daniel vii, 13-14; Psalm lxxxix, 1-37.

CHAPTER XVI

THE RENDING OF THE KINGDOM

Although Israel reached the peak of her prosperity during the reigns of David and Solomon, the seeds of her decline and fall had already been sown. For by her action in rejecting Jehovah as her reigning sovereign, she had exposed herself to the frailty and folly of a human king.

The fame of Solomon's wisdom was, and still is, world wide; nevertheless, in his old age he marred an otherwise glorious reign by allowing idolatry once more to rear its hideous head within the borders of his realm.

In so doing he broke the Law of the Lord and brought

upon the royal house the lash of correction which had been foreshadowed in the Davidic Covenant.

Full of righteous anger the Lord told Solomon that He would reduce his kingdom by tearing away ten tribes out of his hand, thus leaving him to reign over two tribes only; those tribes being the royal tribe of Judah and the little tribe of Benjamin, in whose territory lay the city of Jerusalem.

For David's sake, however, this punishment was not to fall upon Solomon himself, but upon his son Rehoboam, who would thus lose his title of King of Israel and become merely King of Judah.

Read 1 Kings xi, 1-13.

Jeroboam

After this announcement Ahijah the prophet was sent to tell Jeroboam, the son of Nebat, that the Lord was about to take away ten tribes from the House of David, and that he had been selected to reign over these ten tribes under the title of King of Israel.

The offer of a royal dynasty was made to Jeroboam on conditions which he afterwards failed to fulfil; but at the same time he was informed that the punishment of the House of David was not intended to last for all time.

Read 1 Kings xi, 26-40.

The Rebellion

In due course Solomon was succeeded by his son Rehoboam, and the people seized their opportunity to make a loyal petition. Headed by Jeroboam they craved for some relief from the crushing burden of taxation which had been imposed upon them by Solomon.

It would seem, however, that Rehoboam was one of those young men who regard the mere accident of birth as a proof of their own ability. Egged on by a party of young hotheads, Rehoboam rejected the sage advice of his father's counsellors, and so far from granting the people's request, threatened to increase their burdens.

The immediate consequence was the rebellion of all Israel, with the exception of the tribes of Judah and Benjamin. With the famous cry "To your tents, O Israel! Now

74

see to thine own house, David!" the ten tribes of Israel revolted against the House of David and set up their own kingdom under Jeroboam, the son of Nebat.

The Separation Ordained by God

Roused to fury by this unexpected development, Rehoboam called out the armed forces of Judah and Benjamin, and prepared to march against the rebels. But this was not allowed, for God forbade the expedition with the words: "This thing is from Me."

Read 1 Kings xii, 1-24.

Israel and Judah

No phenomenon of modern times is more amazing than the popular idea that Israel and Judah are identical terms.

The origin of this delusion may possibly be found in Ezekiel xi, 15; but its persistence, even in Christian communities, is the more remarkable in face of its obvious absurdity.

The fact remains, however, that belief in this glaring error renders a very large part of the Bible unintelligible; and it is essential that we should have a clear understanding of how these terms originated, and of what they really mean.

Israel, Abraham's grandson, had twelve sons, of whom Judah was one.

Each of these sons founded a tribe, with the exception of Joseph, who founded two tribes through his sons Ephraim and Manasseh. There were, therefore, thirteen tribes of Israel, of which Judah was one.

These thirteen tribes were formed into a kingdom; and each tribe received a suitable grant of territory, with the exception of the tribe of Levi, to which only the revenues of certain cities were allotted. There were, therefore, twelve territorial tribes in the kingdom of Israel, of which Judah was one.

After the rebellion against Rehoboam these twelve territorial tribes were divided into two separate and distinct kingdoms. The tribes of Judah and Benjamin formed the kingdom of Judah, while the remaining ten tribes formed the kingdom of Israel.

From the time of their separation the two kingdoms of Israel and Judah existed side by side for about 250 years, under different kings, with different histories, and in mutual antipathy. Their widely divergent destinies are set forth in the books of the Prophets, where they are continually contrasted under various similes, such as two families, two sisters, two pots, and two sticks.

It should be clear, then, that the tribe of Judah was one tribe and one tribe only, of the twelve territorial tribes of Israel.

It should be clear also that the kingdom of Judah consisted of the territorial tribes of Judah and Benjamin, two tribes, and two tribes only, of the twelve territorial tribes of Israel.

Conversely, it should be equally clear that the ten tribes which formed the kingdom of Israel could not possibly have been Judah.

When, therefore, so-called scholars and others state that Israel and Judah are interchangeable terms, they are disputing what Euclid calls a self-evident truth, and asserting with ridiculous solemnity that the part is equal to the whole.

The Decline of Israel

After his installation as king of Israel, Jeroboam very quickly realised that strict observance of the Law of the Lord was not compatible with the maintenance of his new kingdom as a political entity separate from Judah.

Under the Law, all the men of all the tribes of Israel were required to worship at the Tabernacle three times a year. The Tabernacle had been replaced by the Temple in Jerusalem; and Jerusalem was now the metropolis of Judah.

From a political point of view the continuance of this practice would have been most unwise; firstly, because Judah was furiously angry with Israel, and any such mass invasion, even for religious purposes, would almost certainly have resulted in bloodshed; secondly, because it would have meant a considerable loss of trade; and thirdly, because it was obvious that, while Jerusalem remained the centre of religious worship, the reunion of the two kingdoms under the House of David would always be a dangerous possibility.

The Calves of Gold

Therefore Jeroboam expressly forbade his people to go up to Jerusalem and established two new religious centres, one at Dan in the extreme north, and the other at Bethel in the south. At these two places he set up calves of gold and instituted a debased form of worship, making priests of the lowest of the people.

From that time onward the Law of the Lord fell more and more into disuse, until Omri, the sixth king, swept it aside, and presented Israel with a complete new code, which was afterwards known as the Statutes of Omri.

Read 1 Kings xii, 25-33; Micah vi, 16.

Prophet after prophet was sent by God to plead with the people of the kingdom of Israel, and to warn them of the punishment which would surely follow. But pleading and warning were alike in vain. Israel refused to repent; she rejected her high calling to be a blessing to all the families of the earth; she trampled the Law of the Lord underfoot; and in so doing she broke the Mosaic Covenant.

Read 2 Kings xvii, 7-17.

CHAPTER XVII

THE DEPORTATIONS OF ISRAEL

As we have already seen, the Mosaic Covenant was a conditional covenant which was laid by God before the descendants of Israel, and accepted by them of their own free will.

On the one hand, the Children of Israel undertook to put the Law of the Lord into practice, and to demonstrate it to the Gentiles; on the other hand, God promised certain blessings if they kept their promise, and certain curses, or punishments, if they failed to keep it.

Those punishments included, among other things, banishment from the Promised Land, dispersal among the Gentiles, and "seven times," or 2,520 years, of divine disfavour.

77

All the tribes of Israel broke the Mosaic Covenant, but the decline of Israel was more rapid than that of Judah; and the curse fell first upon the ten-tribed kingdom of Israel.

Assyria

During the eighth century B.C. the kingdom or empire of Assyria, which already occupied a large portion of Central Asia, was making further efforts to extend its boundaries. Israel and Judah, puny by comparison, straddled the caravan routes from Asia Minor to Egypt, and for that reason occupied a very important strategic position; while the seaports on the coastline formed a desirable outlet to the Mediterranean Sea.

Assyria's ambition to bring the land of Canaan under her yoke was now used by God to work out His purposes; and in four successive invasions by the armies of that country, Israel was humiliated, broken, and uprooted from the Promised Land.

First Invasion

In the reign of Menahem, sixteenth king, Israel was invaded by Pul, commander-in-chief of Assurdan III, who afterwards usurped the throne of Assyria under the title of Tiglath-pileser III. Heavy tribute was exacted, but no captives were taken on this occasion.

Read 2 Kings xv, 19-20.

Second Invasion, B.C. 741

In the reign of Pekah, eighteenth king, Israel was again invaded by Tiglath-pileser. The tribes on the east of the Jordan (Reuben, Gad, and half the tribe of Manasseh), together with portions of Naphtali and other tribes in the north, were deported to "Halah and Habor and Hara, and to the river Gozan."

Commenting on this invasion, the Rev. H. A. Edwards writes in his excellent book, *God Omnipotent*:

"There is a book recommended by the authorities of the British Museum, entitled *The Ancient Records of Assyria and Babylonia*; it was published in 1926, and is written by Daniel David Luckenbill, Professor of Semitic Languages and Literature in the University of Chicago. It is one of a series, 'Ancient Records,' published under the general editorship of Professor J. H. Breasted. In this book there is a translation given of an inscription of Tiglath-pileser III which deals with this first deportation mentioned in 2 Kings xv, 29, and which confirms it. This is what the Assyrian inscription says, according to Luckenbill Vol. I, par. 815, p. 292:

" 'The cities of . . . Gala'za, Abilakka, which are on the border of Bit-Humria (House of Omri, Israel) . . . the wide land of Naphtali, in its entirety, I brought within the border of Assyria. My official I set over them as governor. . . .'

"In par. 816 we read further:

" 'The land of Bit-Humria . . . all of its people together with their goods I carried off to Assyria. Pakaha, their king, they deposed, and I placed Ausi' over them as king. Ten talents of gold, ten talents of silver, as their tribute I received from them, and to Assyria I carried them.'

"We note that Luckenbill (under Breasted's editorship) translates Bit-Humria as 'House of Omri, Israel.'

"The names of their kings are given in Assyrian form as Pakaha and Ausi'; obviously the same persons as the Biblical Pekah and Hosea, thus identifying this particular invasion."

Read 2 Kings xv, 29-30; 1 Chronicles v, 26.

Third Invasion, B.C. 721

Hoshea, the nineteenth king, having made an alliance with Egypt, refused to pay tribute to Assyria. Israel was therefore invaded by Shalmaneser V, who took Hoshea prisoner and laid siege to his capital, Samaria.

During the siege, which lasted three years, Shalmaneser died, but his successor, Sargon, captured the city and deported the citizens to Halah and Habor by the river Gozan, and in the cities of the Medes.

Concerning this invasion, the Rev. H. A. Edwards writes:

"Here is the inscription, also to be found in Luckenbill, as well as in *Assyria, its Princes, Priests and People*, by

Professor A. H. Sayce, late Professor of Assyriology of Oxford, on p. 178, 1926 edition:

" '(In the beginning of my reign) the city of Samaria I besieged, I captured . . . 27,280 of its inhabitants I carried away; fifty chariots in the midst of them I collected (and the rest of their goods I seized); I set my governor over them and laid upon them tribute and taxes like those of the Assyrians.

" '(Sargon) the conqueror of the Thamudites, the Ibadidites, the Marsimanites, and the Khapayans, the remainder of whom was carried away and whom he transported to the midst of the land of Beth-Omri.'

"That is, the House of Omri, so called after Omri, who substituted his own laws for the Law of the Lord in the northern kingdom."

Thus the whole country was placed under an Assyrian governor, and Israel ceased to be a kingdom. The inhabitants of the city of Samaria were added to the people who had been deported in the second invasion; and into the regions thus left vacant, Sargon imported families or tribes from other parts of the Assyrian Empire.

Read 2 Kings xvii, 1-6; xviii, 9-12.

Fourth Invasion, B.C. 676

After the third invasion Israel lay broken and helpless, a mere appendage of the great Assyrian Empire. In B.C. 676, however, her territory was again overrun by the Assyrian armies during an expedition by Esar-haddon against Manasseh, king of Judah.

The Biblical account of this invasion, in so far as it affected Israel, is scanty, owing to the fact that the official records of the kingdom of Israel ceased with the fall of Samaria in B.C. 721. But a critical consideration of all the available evidence leads to the conclusion that the deportation of almost all the remainder of the people of Israel took place during this campaign.

Read 2 Chronicles xxxiii, 11; 2 Kings xvii, 18, 22-24.

It should be remembered that, while it was the custom of most ancient conquerors to take large numbers of captives and to enslave them, it was the invariable practice of the

Assyrians to remove all the inhabitants of a conquered territory and to replace them with tribes from other parts of the empire.

The exchange of peoples on this occasion was effected by Esar-haddon.

Read Ezra iv, 1-2.

At the same time, it should be mentioned that, although the record in 2 Kings xvii, 18 states that "there was none left but the tribe of Judah only," some Israelites did manage to escape deportation, or to return; and these were still in the land in the reign of Josiah, king of Judah (B.C. 640-609).

The fate of this small remnant of Israel is not recorded in the Bible, being probably of little interest to the chroniclers of the kingdom of Judah.

Read 2 Chronicles xxxiv, 9.

Arsareth

The beginning of their captivity marks the end of the history of the people of the kingdom of Israel, so far as the Bible is concerned, with the exception of one very important passage in the Apocrypha.

There we read that the ten tribes which were taken captive by Shalmaneser, king of Assyria, in the reign of Hoshea, king of Israel, left the place of their captivity and, crossing the head-waters of the Euphrates, journeyed for eighteen months to a place called Arsareth.

There are good grounds for supposing that the region of Arsareth was a district in the south of Russia, adjacent to the Crimea, and that the route taken by the Israelites was the mountainous defile through the Caucasus, which is known to this day as the Pass of Israel.

Read 2 Esdras xiii, 40-45.

Israel's Continued Exile

No evidence can be produced from any source to show that Israel ever returned to Palestine as a nation, or that any one of the Ten Tribes returned as a tribe.

The fact that there were individual members of some of these tribes in the Holy Land at a later date proves nothing at all. Indeed, it would be just as logical to argue that all our kinsmen of British birth have returned to this country because we can find an Australian, a Canadian, or a South African in London.

In accordance with prophecy, the Ten Tribes of the northern kingdom lost their land, their language, and even their name. They had failed to keep the Mosaic Covenant; they had broken the Third Commandment; they had borne the name of God in vain; and they were no longer fit to be known to the world as Israel, "Ruling with God."

Read Ezekiel xx, 39.

For their iniquity they became as Gentiles among the Gentiles, "aliens from the commonwealth of Israel, and strangers from the covenants of promise, having no hope, and without God in the world."

CHAPTER XVIII

THE DEPORTATIONS OF JUDAH

Meanwhile, the kingdom of Judah, so far from profiting by the lesson of Israel's punishment, was following much the same course. She, too, rejected the Law of the Lord; she, too, adopted the Statutes of Omri; she, too, broke the Mosaic Covenant, and brought upon herself the sentence of banishment.

Read 2 Kings xvii, 19.

The Assyrian Deportation, B.C. 711

In the reign of Hezekiah, the thirteenth king, Judah was invaded by Sennacherib, king of Assyria, who ravaged the land of Judah and took large numbers of prisoners.

A translation of the inscriptions of Sennacherib which bear on this campaign, may be found in the British Museum's publication, *A Guide to Babylonian and Assyrian Antiquities*; the following extract is taken from the 1922 edition, p. 226:

"I then besieged Hezekiah of Judah, who had not submitted to my yoke, and I captured forty-six of his strong cities and fortresses, and innumerable small cities which were round about them, with the battering of rams and the assault of engines, and the attack of foot soldiers, and by mines and breaches (made in the walls).

"I brought out therefrom two hundred thousand and one hundred and fifty people, both small and great, male and female, and horses, and mules, and asses, and camels, and oxen, and innumerable sheep I counted as spoil (Hezekiah) himself, like a caged bird, I shut up within Jerusalem his royal city."

Jerusalem was besieged by Sennacherib, but was miraculously delivered, after king Hezekiah had made humble supplication to the Lord.

The Judahites who were captured during this campaign were, almost certainly, transported to the same region as the Israelites. They never became Jews; and there can be little doubt that in after years they accompanied the Israelites on their migrations.

Read 2 Kings xviii, 13-16.

The Babylonian Deportation, B.C. 606-587

For more than a century the remainder of Judah lived under their own king, and in their own land. Sentence of complete deportation had been suspended in answer to national repentance.

Yet in spite of all warnings, in spite, too, of a notable revival in the reign of the godly young king Josiah, Judah persisted in defying the Law of the Lord. So gross was her idolatry that heathen altars and heathen idols were erected within the very precincts of the Temple itself.

Read Jeremiah iii, 6-11; xxxii, 28-35; 2 Chronicles xxxiii, 1-9; Ezekiel xvi.

Babylon

During this period the Assyrian Empire was succeeded by the Chaldæan Empire of Babylon, and for some time Central Asia was in a state of considerable confusion. Taking advantage of this state of affairs, Necho, Pharaoh of Egypt, led an expedition through Judah, which he reduced to a state of tributary vassalage, and advanced as far as the river Euphrates.

Read 2 Kings xxiii, 29-35.

To meet this menace, Nabopolassar, king of Babylon, collected a large army which he placed under the command of his son Nebuchadnezzar. This brilliant young man drove back the Egyptians, whom he defeated at Carchemish, and proceeded to attack Judah.

In three successive invasions the kingdom of Judah was shattered, Jerusalem was razed to the ground, and the people were taken capitive to Babylon. Only a few peasants were left behind to till the ground for their Chaldæan conquerors.

These three invasions may be summarised as follows:

First Invasion, B.C. 606
In the reign of Jehoiachin.

Read 2 Kings xxiv, 1; 2 Chronicles xxxvi, 5-7.

Second Invasion, B.C. 599
In the reign of Jehoiachin. On this occasion Nebuchadnezzar returned as king, having succeeded his father in B.C. 604.

Read 2 Kings xxiv, 10-16; 2 Chronicles xxxvi, 9-10.

Third Invasion, B.C. 587
In the reign of Zedekiah.

Read 2 Kings xxiv, 17—xxv, 12; 2 Chronicles xxxvi, 11-20.

The Judahites who were captured in these three invasions were all transported to Babylon, where they became known as Jews.

Assyria and Babylon
From an historical point of view the Babylonian deportation of Judah was by far the more important. Even if it could be proved that the Assyrian deportation was the greater numerically, the Babylonian would still have to be regarded as the main deportation.

The captives of the Assyrian deportation drop out of

history as completely as the Israelites. There is no further mention of them in the Bible, except perhaps when the prophet Obadiah refers to "the captivity of Jerusalem which is in Sepharad."

Read Obadiah 20.

On the other hand, a certain number of Judahites of the Babylonian deportation returned to their own land at a later date as Jews, and their history can be traced up to the present day.

CHAPTER XIX

A SHORT RETROSPECT

We have now reached a point in our studies where the descendants of all the sons of Jacob-Israel have broken the Mosaic Covenant, and have, in consequence, been expelled from their native land.

The stage is empty, and the curtain is down, as it were, upon a great epoch in this pageant of national history.

While the stage is being set for the next scene, we may profitably spend a few moments in reviewing the rise and fall of that race which is known in the Bible as the "Children of Israel."

The unconditional promises of the Abrahamic Covenant (that is to say, the responsibility and the equipment for carrying it out) were made to Abraham, confirmed to Isaac, and ratified to Jacob-Israel.

Jacob-Israel's twelve sons founded thirteen tribes, which together formed the people known as the Children of Israel.

At Sinai the Children of Israel were formed into a kingdom, under God Himself as King. This kingdom was the nucleus of God's universal kingdom, the Kingdom of God on earth.

To His newly-formed kingdom, God revealed the eternal principles of righteousness, which He codified in the Law of the Lord.

85

This Law God entrusted to Israel (for demonstration to all mankind) under the Mosaic Covenant, the only condition of which was observance of the Law.

The keeping of this Covenant was to be followed by great blessings; the breaking of the Covenant was to be followed by terrible curses, or punishments, among which was that of expulsion from the Promised Land.

After nearly four hundred years of direct government by God Himself, the people of the kingdom demanded a visible, human king. This was high treason, as the Lord made clear to Samuel in the words: "They have not rejected thee; but they have rejected Me, that I should not reign over them."

Nevertheless the request was granted, and the dynasty of David was established for all time by an unconditional covenant—the Davidic Covenant.

Under David and his son Solomon, the kingdom rose to the greatest height of its prosperity. The Law of the Lord was put into operation; and the blessings of prosperity, physical health, and immunity from defeat in war followed.

Unfortunately, this happy condition of affairs was comparatively short lived. Toward the end of his reign, Solomon introduced the practice of idolatry on a large scale and, for this sin, it was decreed by God that the greater part of the kingdom should be rent out of the hand of his son Rehoboam.

Thus it came to pass that, after Solomon's death, ten of the tribes rebelled and set up their own king, thus forming the new kingdom of Israel; while Rehoboam was left with only two territorial tribes, Judah and Benjamin, who now styled themselves the kingdom of Judah.

These two kingdoms existed side by side for about 250 years, with different kings and different histories, until first Israel, and then Judah, broke the Mosaic Covenant, and brought upon themselves the sentence of banishment to foreign lands.

The differences between the deportations of Israel and Judah should be carefully noted.

Israel was deported in the period B.C. 741-676; Judah was deported, at least seventy years later, in the period B.C. 606-587.

Israel was deported to Halah, Habor, and the cities of the Medes; Judah was deported to Babylon, some 400 or 500 miles to the south of that region.

Israel was deported by the Assyrians; Judah was deported by the Chaldæans.

Thus the two kingdoms of Israel and Judah were deported at different times, to different places, and by different conquerors.

CHAPTER XX

THE PARTIAL RETURN OF JUDAH

Judah's Babylonian captivity, which was, of course, only part of her punishment of "seven times," lasted seventy years, and during that time this section of the people of Judah became known as the Jews.

In B.C. 537 the Chaldæan Empire came under the domination of the Medes and Persians; and one year later, by a decree of Cyrus the Persian, an opportunity was offered to the Jews of returning to their own country.

Read Ezra i, 1-4.

This offer was only partially accepted, large numbers preferring to remain in the land of their captivity under the easy yoke of their new masters. A considerable body of Jews, 42,360 in number, did, however, return to Palestine where they rebuilt the Temple, and for a time observed the Law of the Lord.

Read Ezra ii, 64; Nehemiah vii, 66.

The Reason for the Return

Here once more we clearly see the hand of God at work, developing His Great Plan of Salvation.

Israel and Judah had failed, and failed disgracefully, to carry out His purposes in the earth. Both had broken the Mosaic Covenant; both had forfeited the blessings and incurred the curse of the Covenant; both had brought upon themselves the punishment of divine disfavour and deportation.

Nevertheless, God was incapable of breaking His plighted word. It was necessary that God the Son should come in human flesh to His own specially created people; it was necessary that He should be born into the royal tribe of Judah, and into the royal House of David, at the royal city of Bethlehem.

Therefore a portion of the kingdom of Judah, containing representatives of the lineage of David, was brought back to Palestine, to prepare the world for the Coming of the Messiah.

The Jews in Palestine

Such was the privilege, such the responsibility which was conferred upon this section of the Jews. And yet the history of these people for the next 500 years is one of spiritual decline which manifested itself, not so much in national idolatry, as in a subtle distortion of the Scriptures by false traditions.

From a political point of view, this period was one of turbulent unrest and continuous revolt against the domination of Greece, Egypt, and Syria successively.

In B.C. 63 Palestine was incorporated in the Roman Empire by Pompeius Magnus, as part of the province of Syria.

Herod

At a later date Herod the Great was installed by the Romans as a puppet king. This brilliant, but unscrupulous adventurer, who was not a Jew, but an Idumæan, or Edomite, stopped at nothing in his lust for power. By the ruthless massacre of his opponents, by the murder of his grandfather-in-law, his brother-in-law, and even his own wife and her two sons, he gained for himself a throne, but he failed to win the affection of his people.

Herod's Temple

In the eighteenth year of his reign, B.C. 17, Herod made a great bid for popularity by undertaking the work of rebuilding the Temple of Zerubbabel. This he conceived on such a magnificent scale that the Temple area was inadequate for his design; the site was therefore enlarged to one of about nine acres by building up a wall from the bottom of the valley, and binding huge rocks together with lead and iron.

The Temple proper was built in eighteen months by the priests, but work on other parts of the building was proceeding during our Lord's mortal life. Indeed, the whole structure was not finished till A.D. 64, just six years before it was razed to the ground by the armies of Titus.

CHAPTER XXI

THE MESSIAH

God the Son is the beginning and the end of the Bible, because, as the Second Person of the Triune Majesty, He was God, is God, and ever will be God. Thus He can say of Himself: "I am Alpha and Omega, the beginning and the end, the first and the last."

Read Revelation xxii, 13.

In His special character as the Saviour of the world, He is again the dominant personality of the whole book. He appears in the third chapter of Genesis as the "Seed of the woman," who should bruise the serpent's head, and in the last chapter of Malachi as the "Sun of Righteousness," who should arise with healing in His wings. When we turn to the New Testament we find His name in the first verse of St. Matthew, and also in the last verse of Revelation.

Old Testament Prophecy

Although the Bible is divided into two main parts, He is the central figure of the Old Testament no less than of the New. When He expounded to His disciples in all the Scriptures the things concerning Himself, He began with the books of Moses and went on to the Prophets and the Psalms.

Moses wrote of Him: "The Lord thy God will raise up unto thee a Prophet from the midst of thee, of thy brethren, like unto me; unto Him ye shall hearken"; and from that time onward prophet and psalmist, inspired by the Holy Spirit, unfolded the grandeur of the Messianic theme.

Read Luke xxiv, 27; xxiv, 44-45; John v, 46-47; Acts iii, 22; vii, 37; Deuteronomy xviii, 15-19.

Over and over again the inspired Old Testament writers foretold the Coming of the Saviour; fervently they exhorted their hearers to watch and to prepare; patiently they instructed their readers as to how they might recognise Him when He came.

From this vast storehouse of divine revelation we can select only a few examples.

The Messiah was to be miraculously conceived by a virgin of the royal tribe of Judah and of the royal House of David. He was to be born at Bethlehem in Judæa. He was to be a great teacher, and a great healer. He was to be sold for thirty pieces of silver, and that money was to be used to buy a field from a potter. His body was to be pierced, but not a single bone of it was to be broken; and after His death He was to rise again from the dead.

All these predictions, and very many more, Jesus fulfilled to the letter.

The Anointed One

If Jesus of Nazareth was not the Messiah, then He has no right to the title of Christ, for the Greek word "Christ" is the equivalent of the Hebrew word "Messiah," and both words mean "The Anointed One." The Old Testament authors naturally used the Hebrew word, Messiah, while the New Testament authors, writing in Greek, just as naturally used the Greek word, Christ.

This title, it is important to remember, has a twofold meaning: the Anointed Priest and the Anointed King. As we shall see later, the Lord Jesus combines in His own person both these offices, as Head of Church and State. He came nearly 2,000 years ago in humiliation and abasement as the Anointed Priest, to sacrifice His own body for the sins of the world; He will come again in the future with power and great glory, as the Anointed King.

It is of the utmost importance that we should distinguish clearly between these two functions of the Messiah; for the failure to make this distinction was largely responsible for the rejection of the Messiah by the Jews, and the same failure is largely responsible for the rejection of the Messiah by the world to-day.

The failure of 2,000 years ago, and the failure of to-day, have the same effect—the rejection of the Messiah; but between the two there is one amazing and paradoxical point of difference. Whereas the Jews were watching for the Coming of the Anointed King, and few recognised Him as the Anointed Priest, Christians of to-day recognise the Messiah as the Anointed Priest, but comparatively few are watching for His Coming as the Anointed King.

CHAPTER XXII

THE ANOINTED PRIEST

(I). HIS LIFE AND MINISTRY

*　　*　　*　　*

As we are still endeavouring to trace the historic development of God's Great Plan of Salvation, we must postpone the consideration of the Messiah as the Anointed King to a later chapter, and confine our studies for the present to His function as the Anointed Priest.

Palestine under the Romans

With one brief exception the earthly ministry of our Lord was conducted entirely within the borders of the Holy Land. It is therefore desirable that we should have before us at least a rough idea of the political geography of the country at this time.

Palestine during the Roman occupation comprised land on both sides of the river Jordan, and formed part of the province of Syria. Of the districts into which it was divided, by far the most important were those three which were bounded on the east by the river Jordan, and on the west by the Mediterranean Sea.

Galilee, called after the inland sea of that name, lay in the north; Judæa, containing the city of Jerusalem, lay in the south; while between the two stretched Samaria, which took its title from the ancient capital of the kingdom of Israel.

Samaria

The inhabitants of Samaria were the descendants of those colonists who had been imported from the Assyrian Empire to fill the places of the deported people of the kingdom of Israel. They did not go up to Jerusalem for the religious festivals and, indeed, would not have been welcome there; but they did worship Jehovah in their own fashion at their own temple on Mount Gerizim.

All Jews were expressly forbidden by their leaders to have any dealings of any kind with the Samaritans, except in so far as it might be incumbent upon them to purchase food or other necessities when passing through their territory.

Galileans and Jews

Thus Galilee and Judæa were separated from each other by a wide tract of land which was inhabited by an alien and ostracised people.

This separation resulted in a divergence of manners, customs, speech, and ideals, which caused the Jews of Galilee to fear the Jews of Judæa for their political and religious power, and which led the Jews of Judæa to despise the Jews of Galilee for their provincialism.

In this way it came to pass that the Jews of Galilee called themselves Galileans, while the Jews of Judæa retained the name of Jews or Judæans.

This distinction should be borne in mind when reading the New Testament; and it should be remembered that the term "Jews" is frequently used in its restricted sense of "Judæans."

The Incarnation

Such, in barest outline, was the state of Palestine when God the Son came to this earth in human flesh, being miraculously born of a pure virgin by the "overshadowing" of the Holy Spirit.

Although the birth of Jesus passed unnoticed by the world at large, it caused great excitement in the Holy Land. Bethlehem was full to overflowing at that time with a concourse of people from all parts of the country, and the shepherds must have gossiped with all and sundry about their wonderful experiences. But the great event was also advertised throughout the land in a very unusual way.

Read Luke ii, 1-20.

The Wise Men

The prime cause of this publicity was the arrival in Jerusalem of a camel caravan. This, to be sure, was no uncommon sight in the streets of the capital, where merchandise was constantly arriving from Damascus, Egypt, and the interior of the continent.

The owners of this particular caravan were, however, not merchants, but certain learned astrologers, who had divined from the stars the birth of a Personage so great that they must needs set out across the desert to do Him homage.

Unlike the usual traveller they were in quest, not of commerce, but of information. "Where," they said, "is He that is born King of the Jews? For we have seen His star in the east, and are come to worship Him."

Herod

A strange question this. The Jews had had no king since their return from Babylon. Only in recent times had Herod, the Idumæan adventurer, persuaded the Romans to set him up as their puppet. Unpopular, and an alien, he might be, but he was nevertheless building a magnificent temple; and as for an heir, he had several sons, any one of whom might be expected to succeed him.

Not only were Herod and his court disturbed by this question, but all Jerusalem was thrown into a ferment. In

93

his perplexity Herod sent for the chief priests and scribes, who read out the appropriate prophecy concerning the Messiah's birth at Bethlehem.

The Murder of the Innocents

Then followed what is, perhaps, the most callous massacre in all history. Herod, alarmed for the safety of his somewhat rickety throne, ordered the execution of all babies of two years old and under in Bethlehem and the surrounding district.

The news of this appalling atrocity must have travelled from end to end of Palestine; and the reason for it, the birth of the long-expected Messiah, must have been equally well known.

Read Micah v, 2; Matthew ii.

John the Baptist

Nearly thirty years later the Jews were forcibly reminded of these things, for John the Baptist appeared on the bank of the river Jordan with the startling challenge: "Repent, for the Kingdom of Heaven is at hand."

Popular excitement flared up once more; and as the news spread that he was announcing the imminent coming of the Messiah, the people flocked to him in great numbers, and were baptised in the Jordan confessing their sins.

Read Matthew iii, 1-6; Mark i, 1-8; Luke iii, 1-6; Malachi iii, 1; Isaiah xl, 3-5.

The Tradition of the Elders

All this was in accordance with prophecy, and the Jews should have understood that the Messiah was coming as the Anointed Priest to redeem His people Israel, and to save all mankind by the sacrifice of His own life. But so grossly had the Scriptures been distorted that they had formed an entirely erroneous idea of His mission.

Forgetting, or perhaps ignoring, the fact that they were a very small portion of the whole race of Israel, the Jews were expecting the arrival of a military conqueror who should deliver them from alien oppression and revive the ancient glories of the kingdom of David for their own exclusive benefit.

The origin of this teaching, and the demonstration of its falsity, may be found in the Old Testament.

Read Ezekiel xi, 14-21.

The Ministry of Jesus

When Jesus began His ministry the enthusiasm knew no bounds. He announced Himself as the Messiah and the Son of God, and wherever He went He laid hands on the sick and suffering and healed them. His fame soon spread, and the people flocked to Him in thousands from all parts of Palestine on both banks of the Jordan.

The civil and religious authorities in Jerusalem sent deputation after deputation to interview Him. Remembering the visit of the Wise Men and the preaching of John the Baptist, they saw before them a young man, thirty years old, of perfect physique and great force of character; a member, not only of the tribe of Judah, but also of the House of David, whose birth had taken place at Bethlehem.

They found, moreover, that this young man was performing miracles of healing on a scale which had never before been known, or even imagined.

All this was certainly in accordance with prophecy, but His teaching puzzled them. He had apparently received no religious or military training; and so far from inciting the people to revolt, He was actually preaching peace and submission to authority.

Chief Priests, Scribes and Pharisees

Meanwhile, the common people heard Him gladly; and as His influence continued to increase, the authorities were faced with the dilemma of either admitting His claims or rejecting them.

Read Mark xii, 37.

The Pharisees came to Him, and He denounced them for misleading the people. The priests came to Him, and He denounced them for misinterpreting the Scriptures. The scribes came to Him, and He denounced them for distorting

95

the Law of the Lord. To crown all this, He was preaching the restoration of the Kingdom of God, not to the Palestinian Jews only, but to all Israel.

As time went on, it became more and more evident that they could not make a tool of Him; He was far too honest and uncompromising for that. If they admitted His claims at all they would have to take service under Him and obey His commands.

In these circumstances the priests foresaw the loss of the lucrative business which they had built up in the sale of Temple money, and sacrificial beasts and birds from the Temple farms. The scribes foresaw the loss of their wealth, and possibly of their very livelihood. The Pharisees foresaw the loss of their prestige and political power. They were forced to make their choice between self-interest on the one hand and the Messiah on the other.

A Mysterious Power

Nor was this all. The Bible narrative more than suggests the presence of some sinister force which from the very first denied His claims, derided His teaching, and poisoned the mind of the people against Him.

Whatever this force may have been, it undoubtedly exerted a powerful influence upon the whole nation. Again and again we read that many believed on Him, but did not confess Him openly for fear of the Jews (Judæans).

Even the members of the Sanhedrin did not dare to incur the displeasure of this force. "Nevertheless," we read, "among the chief rulers also many believed on Him; but because of the Pharisees, they did not confess Him, lest they should be put out of the synagogue."

Read John xii, 42-43.

The Decision of the Authorities

Thus the full strength of the civil and religious organisations of the Judæans was pitted against this one man. As He would not be silenced, He would have to be put out of the way; if they could not incite the mob to stone Him to death He would have to be murdered as secretly as possible.

Nicodemus, a secret follower of Jesus, and a member of

96

the Sanhedrin, protested against this course, and advocated a fair trial in accordance with the Law of the Lord; but his intervention was treated with ridicule.

Read John vii, 45-53.

Time after time Jesus escaped out of their hands and, fully conscious of His danger, went calmly to and fro preaching the good news of the Kingdom of God, and healing all who came to Him.

For three whole years He endured the bitterest persecution; and then, with death ever stalking at His heels, He made His way southward to Jerusalem for the last time.

CHAPTER XXIII

THE ANOINTED PRIEST

(II). HIS CRUCIFIXION

The Raising of Lazarus

During the closing days of His all-too-short life, Jesus received a message from His friends Mary and Martha of Bethany, to say that their brother Lazarus was dangerously ill. The little family at Bethany were, of course, some of our Lord's dearest friends, and yet He made no move to answer their appeal; on the contrary, He deliberately waited until the body of Lazarus had been laid in the tomb for four days.

The death of His friend was to be used "for the glory of God, that the Son of God might be glorified thereby." In other words, Jesus was about to give to the Jews one last great conclusive proof that He was indeed the Great Healer, the Messiah, the Christ.

In the course of His ministry He had performed many miracles; He had on several occasions raised the dead; but never before had He, or any other man, brought a human being back from the grave after corruption had set in.

When at last Jesus reached the house of mourning, Martha

and Mary were mildly reproachful: "Lord," they said, "if Thou hadst been here, my brother had not died," Their friends were equally mystified, and said one to another: "Could not this man, which opened the eyes of the blind, have caused that even this man should not have died?"

Martha, at the last moment, even attempted to prevent the apostles from rolling away the stone which blocked the mouth of the cave: "Lord, by this time he stinketh; for he hath been dead four days." But at the command of Jesus the corrupted tissues were suffused with blood, the spirit returned to the body, and Lazarus was restored to the full vigour of life.

Excitement in Jerusalem

It was not long before the news of this, the greatest miracle of all time, was being tossed from mouth to mouth in the streets of Jerusalem, which was only two miles distant.

The city was rapidly filling up with the huge crowd of worshippers who were arriving for the Passover, not only from Palestine itself, but from all the surrounding countries; and already Jews from Rome, Greece, Asia Minor, Central Asia and Egypt were beginning to jostle one another in its narrow ways.

Sightseers poured out of Jerusalem to see for themselves the man who had been raised from the tomb, and to hear the story of the miracle from the lips of Mary and Martha.

Alarm of the Authorities

Jesus became the hero of the hour; but He was nowhere to be found. Nevertheless, the authorities were genuinely alarmed, and they even considered the advisability of destroying the chief evidence of the miracle by putting Lazarus to death.

With such a concourse of people in the city, many of them disciples of Jesus from Galilee, it was impossible to foresee what might happen. At any moment the mob might attack the Roman garrison and set Jesus up as king; in which case Rome would hold the Sanhedrin responsible, and impose the severest penalties on the whole nation.

The Sanhedrin

Accordingly a meeting of the Sanhedrin was convened, at which it was decided to effect the murder of Jesus as speedily as possible.

Read John xi, 1-54.

It must not be supposed that the decision to murder Jesus was absolutely unanimous. Joseph of Arimathæa was certainly not one of those who voted for His death, and there were probably one or two others who followed his example. Among them we may imagine the following: Jairus, whose daughter had been raised from the dead; the rich young ruler, who knelt to Jesus; Nicodemus, a secret disciple; and possibly that wise old man Gamaliel.

Read Luke xxiii, 50-51.

Nevertheless, the majority against Jesus must have been overwhelming, and the fact remains that the resolution to effect His murder was formally passed by the supreme National Council.

The Triumphal Entry into Jerusalem

Five days before the Passover the very development which the Judæan authorities were dreading actually took place. Jesus, having spent the night with Lazarus, set out from Bethany for Jerusalem; on the way He was met by a large crowd which escorted Him into the city like a king entering into his capital.

Read John xii, 9-19.

This demonstration in favour of Jesus placed the authorities in a very awkward predicament. If, on the one hand, they arrested Jesus they might themselves be in danger from the mob; if, on the other hand, they failed to arrest Him the people might "take Jesus by force and make Him a king," as they had wished to do on a previous occasion. In either case there would be rioting and bloodshed for which Rome would hold them responsible.

Read John vi, 14-15.

Faced with this dilemma the Judæans decided that they must shelter themselves behind the power of Rome. If they could only arrest Jesus without danger to themselves, and give Him some semblance of legal trial, they could then take Him to Pilate and demand His instant execution on the ground that they had found Him guilty of leading an insurrection.

Judas

It was at this juncture that Judas Iscariot went to the chief priests and offered to show them how Jesus might be arrested in absolute secrecy. Needless to say, his offer was accepted; but the opportunity to make use of it did not occur till the following Thursday, which was the Feast of the Passover.

The Last Supper

On that day Jesus celebrated the Passover with His Apostles, and instituted the feast of the Lord's Supper in its place.

Gethsemane

After supper He led the Apostles, all except Judas Iscariot, through one of the city gates on to the slopes of the Mount of Olives, where He entered a garden, or orchard, near the little village of Gethsemane.

This was a favourite retreat of His, and here He endured the greatest temptation of His life. In the thing which He had to do on the morrow, not even the Father could help Him; He must tread the winepress of the wrath of God in utter loneliness, with all the forces of evil arrayed against Him.

Even then, it was not too late to turn back had He wished to do so. "Thinkest thou," He asked Peter, "that I cannot now pray to the Father, and He shall presently give Me more than twelve legions of angels? But how then shall the Scriptures be fulfilled, that thus it must be?"

Read Matthew xxvi, 53-54

The success, or failure, of God's Great Plan of Salvation depended upon Him, and upon Him alone. For the redemption of His people Israel He must not fail; for the salvation of all mankind He must endure to the bitter end.

Never was any man faced with such appalling responsibility; never was any man asked to pay so terrible a price; and never did any man achieve a greater, or more glorious, victory.

The Arrest

When the agony of the temptation was over, Judas arrived with a large company, chief priests, elders, and a detachment of Judæan soldiers from the Temple Guard. Jesus had often eluded His would-be assassins before, but this time the authorities were determined that He should not escape, even in the darkness. To make sure of this, they arranged that Judas should hold Jesus in his embrace while the soldiers seized Him from behind.

As this company picked its way through the orchard by the light of lanterns and torches, flight would probably have been an easy matter, but Jesus made no move. Calmly He announced His presence; patiently He endured the kiss of His betrayer; willingly He allowed Himself to be bound, and smuggled into Jerusalem.

The Crucifixion

During all that followed, Jesus maintained the same unflinching courage and the same majestic dignity.

While the priests and the council were slandering and humiliating Him; while the spit of the scum of Jerusalem was trickling down His cheeks; while the whips of the Roman soldiers raised great livid weals upon His back; while they mocked Him, and forced the crown of thorns upon His brow; while He staggered beneath the weight of the cross; while they hammered great nails into His hands and feet; when they hoisted Him up like a felon, between two other felons, He never forgot that the success, or failure, of God's Great Plan of Salvation depended upon His courage, His endurance and, above all, upon His faith in the Father.

101

The Agony of the Cross

It was not, however, the torture of the flesh which broke His heart, but the infinitely greater torture of the spirit. *He had lived a life of perfect purity*, in the closest communion with the Father. *Not for a single moment had He known the shame and the degradation of evil, nor the pain of God's displeasure.*

Yet He took upon Himself the sins of all mankind, past, present and future; and not only the sins, but all those diseases of body and soul which are the consequences of sin. In His all-embracing love He drew upon Himself all the pollution and the defilement which He abhorred, and which must inevitably come between Him and the Father.

Cut off, as it were, by that thunder-cloud of sin, Jesus was lone in the hour of death; and the agony of separation wrung from His lips the awful cry: "My God, My God, why hast Thou forsaken Me?"

The Darkness

The manifestation of Evil was so terrible that there was darkness over all the land for three hours from midday onwards.

The Burial

Soon after three in the afternoon the lifeless body of Jesus was taken down from the cross and laid by Joseph of Arimathæa in his own new, rock-hewn tomb. The entrance to the tomb was closed by a great stone, which was sealed by the priests and guarded by their soldiers.

The whole ghastly travesty of justice had lasted only some twelve hours. Jesus was arrested sometime before dawn; by midday He had been nailed to the cross; and by three o'clock in the afternoon He was dead.

Chapter XXIV

THE ANOINTED PRIEST

(III). HIS RESURRECTION AND ASCENSION

The Descent into Hell

For the time being, the drama was over in Jerusalem; but it continued in the spirit world. In His great work of redemption Jesus had paid the price of death physical; He had yet to pay the greater price of death spiritual; for only so could He buy back for man that immortal body which man had lost in Eden.

While His body lay in the tomb, securely guarded against any possible interference, His spirit went down to Hell, the place of departed spirits, or the place of the spirits in prison.

Read 1 Peter iii, 18-20.

The Prison-house of the Dead

St. Peter's expression, "spirits in prison," implies the detention of those departed spirits, against their will, in a place of confinement, by some person empowered to keep them there.

Strangely enough, the New Testament has little to say about this particular phase in the mortal life of Jesus, but St. Peter gives us a very clear indication as to where we may look for further light on the matter.

Prophetic Psalms

Peter was present with the other Apostles when Jesus opened their understanding that they might understand all those things which were written in the Law of Moses, and in the Prophets, and in the Psalms concerning Him; and he asserts, with all the certainty of the knowledge which was then imparted to him, that Psalm xvi is prophetic of the Messiah and, indeed, records His very words: "My flesh also shall rest in hope. For Thou wilt not leave My soul in Hell; neither wilt Thou suffer Thine Holy One to see curruption."

Read Luke xxiv, 44-45; Acts ii, 25-31; Psalm xvi, 8-11.

When we ourselves turn to the Psalms, we find that some of them foretell the life and death of Jesus with amazing and vivid accuracy. Psalm xxii is such a psalm, opening, as it does, with the exact words of the Messiah's agonised cry from the cross: "My God, My God, why hast Thou forsaken Me?" Even a slight acquaintance with these prophetic psalms forces us to the conclusion that, while the pen may be the pen of David, or of some other psalmist, the voice is the voice of God the Son.

Read Psalm xxii.

Further study reveals the fact that other psalms describe the descent of Jesus to the prison-house of the dead, His helplessness in the power of the arch-enemy, His prayers for deliverance, and His faith that the Father would effect His rescue.

Read Psalm lxxxviii; cxlii; cxliii; lxxxvi; cxvi, 1-9.

The Deliverance

By entering the prison-house of the dead, Jesus accomplished the purpose for which He came into the world. And when He called to the Father, "Deliver Me from My persecutors; for they are stronger than I. Bring My soul out of prison, that I may praise Thy name," the Lord heard from Heaven and delivered Him.

Read Psalm xviii, 1-24.

Thus, by passing through death, Jesus gained the victory over Death, and opened the way to everlasting life. No longer need man fear his last journey into the unknown, for the keys of Hell had been taken away from Satan, and had been handed for ever to the Saviour of the world.

Read Hebrews ii, 14-15; Revelation i, 12-18.

The Resurrection

In the meantime the body of Jesus lay in the new tomb which Joseph of Arimathæa had hewn out of the rock for himself.

The chief priests and the Pharisees, although they had satisfied themselves that Jesus was actually dead, and had seen the mouth of the tomb blocked by a great stone, were nevertheless very nervous lest Jesus should fulfil His prophecy and rise from the dead on the third day.

In their alarm they went to Pilate and demanded a guard of Roman soldiers. When this was refused they themselves sealed the entrance to the cave, and posted their own guard of Judæan soldiers, or police.

Very early in the morning of the third day the spirit of Jesus returned to His body; that body was changed from a mortal body to an immortal body; and Jesus came back to this world, the first man to rise from the dead to everlasting life.

Amid all the terrors of a great earthquake, an angel rolled back the stone from the mouth of the cave, disclosing the fact that the body of Jesus was no longer there.

Certain women, who had set out under cover of darkness, approached the tomb in the hope that they might be able to enter and to perform the last offices for the dead. To their amazement and joy these women met the Risen Lord Himself, and ran back to tell the Apostles.

The Bribing of the Soldiers

At the same time the Judæan police, who had been paralysed by fright, hurried into the city and reported to the priests exactly what had happened. A meeting of the Sanhedrin was hastily summoned, and the police were bribed to say that the disciples of Jesus had stolen His body while they were asleep.

John's Realisation of the Truth

Peter and John were the first Apostles to enter the empty tomb, and the record tells us that Peter "departed wondering," while John "saw and believed." Undoubtedly John believed that his Lord and Master had risen from the dead, and he believed because he saw. But what did he see to convince him that Jesus had risen?

Burial Customs of the Jews

In order to understand just what the scene inside the

tomb conveyed to John, we must know something of the burial customs of the time, which differed considerably from those of the present day.

After death the body was first washed and then wrapped round and round with long, broad bandages from the neck down to the feet. The folds of these bandages overlapped one another, strapping the arms securely to the sides, and binding the legs firmly together. During the winding, spices were poured in between the folds of the bandages.

A napkin, or piece of linen, was folded and tied round the head in such a way as to make a bandage or cap. The face was left exposed.

Burial almost invariably took place on the day of death; and, when circumstances permitted, the body was not buried in the earth, but was placed in a cavity cut out of the rock, with an entrance at the side or end.

The nature of the material which was used for the bandages, the weight and quality of the spices, and the type of sepulchre, depended on the circumstances of the relatives.

For the burial of Jesus, Nicodemus brought about one hundred pounds weight of myrrh and aloes; the wrappings were of fine linen; and the tomb was a rock-hewn cave undefiled by death. Thus, having died between two common felons, Jesus was nevertheless accorded a rich man's funeral, in strict fulfilment of prophecy.

Read Isaiah liii, 9.

The Scene in the Tomb

When John entered the tomb he saw the linen bandages still lying there, almost as if the body were inside them, and the stiff linen cap standing up just where the head had been.

This sight convinced John that Jesus had risen from the dead. He probably saw the explanation in a moment, but we, too, may arrive at the same conclusion by following out his line of reasoning.

The Evidence of the Empty Tomb

One fact, at any rate, was beyond dispute: there was no body in the tomb, and the bandages lying there before his eyes had obviously contained a body quite recently.

Had Jesus Really Died?

Yes. There were scores of witnesses, and one soldier had made certain of His death by thrusting a spear under His ribs and up into His heart.

Had He been Buried in the Tomb?

Yes. Joseph of Arimathæa and Nicodemus had seen to that; and two women, whom he knew well, had witnessed the burying. Besides, the priests and Pharisees had made very certain that the dead body of Jesus was inside the tomb before they had sealed the entrance and set a guard upon it.

Supposing that Jesus was not really Dead, could He have regained Consciousness in the Tomb and made His Escape?

No. He could not have freed His arms from the bandages; and even if He had, He would still have had to unwind the wrappings from His body and legs before He could have moved about.

Had He been helped to Escape?

No. If He had, then the bandages would have been cut or unwrapped, and left in disorder, or else taken away altogether.

Had the Body been stolen?

No. Any one wishing to steal the body would have had to adopt one of three courses: (*a*) to unwind the bandages and leave them behind; (*b*) to cut the bandages and leave them behind; (*c*) to take the bandages away with the body.

The body could not have been stolen because the bandages lay there before his eyes uncut, undisturbed, each fold in its place just as they had been wrapped round the body, except that the folds had sunk down beneath the great weight of the spices.

How, then had the Body disappeared?

There was only one explanation. Jesus had risen from the dead, with His body transformed in such a way that it could free itself from bandages and head-dress without disarranging them.

Appearances of the Risen Lord

It was not long before Jesus made Himself known, first to Mary Magdalene, then to Cleopas and another disciple on the way to Emmaus, shortly afterwards to the eleven apostles, and later still to more than five hundred brethren at once.

The Immortal Body

He could disguise His personality, for Mary Magdalene took Him for a gardener, and the two disciples on the way to Emmaus did not recognise Him until He broke bread with them. He could appear and disappear at will, passing, when He wished to do so, through stone walls and locked doors.

Yet His body was a real body, bearing the marks of the nails in the hands and feet, and the gash of the spear in the side. It was the same body, but changed from mortality to immortality; the body of the first man to rise from the dead to everlasting life.

Read Matthew xxvii, 57—xxviii, 15; Mark xv, 42—xvi, 8; Luke xxiv, 1-48; John xix, 31—xx; 1 Corinthians xv, 6.

The Forty Days

For nearly six weeks Jesus remained on this earth demonstrating the immortal body which He had regained for man, and instructing the Apostles in the Gospel which they were to preach to all nations.

The Ascension

At the end of the forty days He ascended into Heaven taking with Him His immortal body, or as the Athanasian Creed puts it, "taking the Manhood into God." There He is, at one and the same time, "perfect God and perfect Man," the great Anointed Priest of all mankind, waiting until the time shall come for Him to return as the Anointed King.

Read Acts i, 1-11; 1 John ii, 1-2; Hebrews vii, 24-28; Acts iii, 19-21.

The Messiah's Mission as the Anointed Priest

As we have already seen, the title of the Messiah, or the

108

Christ, has a twofold meaning: the Anointed Priest and the Anointed King.

. God the Son came to this earth nearly 2,000 years ago in the first of these capacities, as the Anointed Priest, and the object of His coming on that occasion is revealed to us in His own words: "The Son of Man is come to seek and to save that which was lost."

These words are almost identical with those which He had spoken through the mouth of the prophet Ezekiel nearly 600 years before: "I will seek that which was lost."

The Redeemer of Israel

The Ten Tribes of the kingdom of Israel had been driven out by God and scattered among the Gentiles; they had become the Lost Sheep of the House of Israel, and to these lost sheep the Lord God had made His promise.

"Behold I, even I, will both search My sheep, and seek them out.

"As a shepherd seeketh out his flock in the day that he is among his sheep that are scattered, so will I seek out My sheep, and will deliver them out of all places where they have been scattered in the cloudy and dark day.

"I will seek that which was lost, and bring again that which was driven away."

Read Ezekiel xxxiv, 11-16.

God the Son came, then, to redeem the Lost Sheep of the House of Israel, and to bring them back, as a nation, into covenant relationship with Himself.

The Saviour of the World

The redemption of Israel was, however, part of an even greater purpose.

By the sin of Adam in the Garden of Eden, mankind had lost the perfect immortal body, and this could only be regained by the incarnation, death, and resurrection of God the Son Himself.

In coming as the Anointed Priest, therefore, the Messiah came, at one and the same time, to be the Redeemer of Israel and the Saviour of the world.

Chapter XXV

THE REDEEMER OF ISRAEL

Six months before the birth of Jesus, Zacharias, a priest of the Temple in Jerusalem, uttered a remarkable prophecy; this was made over the cradle of his week-old son, John the Baptist, and was addressed to him, although it spoke mainly of the Messiah, whose forerunner he was to be.

Delivered, as it was, under the direct inspiration of the Holy Spirit, this prophecy summed up in a remarkable manner those great truths which the Lord God of Israel had been proclaiming through the mouth of His holy prophets since the world began.

Not once, nor twice, but hundreds of times the Lord God had announced His intention of redeeming His people Israel, in order that they might fulfil their mission and carry out His purposes in the earth.

Read Luke i, 57-80; Isaiah liv, 4-8; xliv, 21-23.

The Curse of the Law

Under the Abrahamic Covenant Israel had been formed into a nation for the express purpose of bringing the world to the knowledge of God, and thereby to the observance of His holy laws.

Those laws had been codified at Sinai, and had been delivered into the keeping of Israel as a sacred trust for all mankind. So sacred was this trust that a special Covenant, relating to Israel, was incorporated in the Law.

Under this Covenant, commonly known as the Mosaic Covenant, Israel undertook, for her part, to demonstrate the Law of the Lord to other nations by first putting it into practice herself; while God, for His part, guaranteed to Israel certain blessings if she kept the Covenant, and certain curses, or punishments, if she broke it. Thus Israel was offered the free choice of earning either the blessing or the curse of the Mosaic Covenant.

This Covenant in no way abolished or invalidated the

Abrahamic Covenant, but was, on the contrary, subservient to it. The Abrahamic Covenant was unconditional; the Mosaic Covenant, on the other hand, was conditional, and was "added" to the Abrahamic Covenant because of the sins of Israel, in order that it might be her schoolmaster to bring her to Christ.

After the great split in the reign of Rehoboam, first the kingdom of Israel, and then the kingdom of Judah, broke the Mosaic Covenant by rejecting the Law of the Lord. In so doing they not only forfeited the blessing, but brought upon themselves the curse of the Covenant which had been incorporated in the Law.

From this curse, described by St. Paul as the Curse of the Law, the Messiah redeemed His people Israel by taking that curse upon Himself.

Read Galatians iii, 7-26.

The New Covenant

As the Redeemer of Israel, Jesus introduced the New Covenant, or New Testament, and sealed it with His blood.

Read Matthew xxvi, 26-28.

The terms of the New Covenant had been revealed by the Lord through the mouth of His prophet Jeremiah some 600 years before. From that revelation we learn that this Covenant was to be made, not with the Gentiles as many suppose, but with the House of Israel and the House of Judah, in substitution for the Mosaic Covenant.

Read Jeremiah xxxi, 31-37.

The very words of the Lord by the mouth of Jeremiah are quoted in the Epistle to the Hebrews as the terms of the New Covenant which was introduced by the Messiah. The author refers to the Mosaic Covenant as the "first covenant," and says that Jesus is the mediator of a better covenant, the New Covenant, which is established upon better promises; the better promises being, of course, the "promises made to the fathers" in the Abrahamic Covenant.

Thus the Messiah came to make a new national covenant with the House of Israel and the House of Judah in place of the Mosaic Covenant, which they had broken.

111

Like the Mosaic Covenant, which it replaced, this New Covenant is "established upon," or an extension of, the "better," or unconditional, promises of the Abrahamic Covenant. Unlike the Mosaic Covenant, the New Covenant is unconditional; its terms are not "if" and "but," but "I will" and "they shall."

By His action in introducing the New Covenant, Jesus brought the Mosaic Covenant to an end, and made it the Old Covenant. It is from this fact that the major divisions of the Bible derive their names; for the New Testament is the book of the New Covenant in Christ Jesus, while the Old Testament is the book of the Old, or Mosaic, Covenant.

Read Hebrews viii.

Israel's Mission Restored

Under the Old Covenant Israel had been separated from the nations of the world to be a chosen people, an holy nation, a kingdom of priests, and a peculiar treasure above all people to God Himself.

Read Exodus xix, 5-6; Deuteronomy x, 15; xiv, 2.

For her sin in breaking this Covenant Israel had been cast off by God; she had become Lo-ruhamah (not having found mercy), and Lo-ammi (not my people). But even while pronouncing this sentence, God had made the great promise: "It shall come to pass that in the place where it was said unto them, ye are not My people, there it shall be said unto them, ye are the sons of the living God. I will have mercy upon her that had not obtained mercy; and I will say to them which were not My people, Thou art My people; and they shall say, Thou art my God."

Read Hosea i, 6-10; ii, 23.

In sealing the New Covenant with His life-blood, Jesus restored Israel once more to the position of a nation set apart for His service.

Thus St. Peter, writing to the "Elect according to the foreknowledge of God the Father," was able to tell Israelites "scattered throughout Pontus, Galatia, Cappadocia, Asia and Bithynia," that by the death and resurrection of their

112

Redeemer, they had "obtained mercy," and had again become "a chosen generation, a royal priesthood, an holy nation, and a peculiar people."

Read 1 Peter ii, 9-10.

The New Covenant and the Gentiles

Although it is true to say that the New Covenant was made with Israel and Judah, there is one very important aspect in which this covenant is extended to the Gentiles.

As we have seen, the race of Israel was created by God to found a kingdom for Himself. This kingdom was capable of infinite expansion, and was designed to be the basis of the Kingdom of God, or Kingdom of Heaven, on earth.

The vocation of the kingdom was to practise and teach the whole counsel of God in both its interdependent and inseparable parts; that is to say, the Gospel of the Kingdom and the Gospel of Salvation.

The decline of the Kingdom into two kingdoms under human kings, and their utter failure to live up to their great vocation, led to the temporary rejection of the whole race of Israel, the House of Israel and the House of Judah, from divine favour.

Nevertheless the purposes of God were not to be defeated by the frailties of man. In due time God, in the person of the only-begotten Son, came into the world to redeem His people for Himself, and to make with them a New Covenant under which they might resume the responsibilities of the Kingdom of Heaven on earth.

The redemption of the people who had been created to declare the whole counsel of God was, of course, part of a greater plan, the salvation of the whole world. By His great victory over Satan and Death, Jesus offers individual salvation from spiritual death to all those who will receive it from Him. In this matter of personal salvation there is no distinction of race, social position, or sex; Israelite, Jew and Gentile alike must look to the Saviour for this priceless gift.

In accepting that gift the Israelite resumes the responsibility to declare the whole counsel of God which was laid upon his race in the Abrahamic Covenant; the Gentile assumes the same responsibility by the grace of the Lord Jesus.

Thus by grace the Christian Gentile takes upon himself the racial responsibility of the Seed of Abraham; and for this reason he becomes the seed of Abraham by adoption, an inheritor of the Abrahamic Covenant, and a citizen of the Kingdom of Heaven on earth.

Read Ephesians ii, 11-19; Galatians iii, 26-29.

It is obvious, then, that the redemption of Israel is a matter of the very highest importance to all mankind. For only by faith in this act of divine mercy can Israelite, Jew and Gentile sing together in praise of their Redeemer: "When Thou hadst overcome the sharpness of death, Thou didst open the Kingdom of Heaven to all believers."

CHAPTER XXVI

THE SAVIOUR OF THE WORLD

Because it has been assumed, quite erroneously, that the Book of the New Testament teaches only the major Gospel of Personal Salvation to the exclusion of the minor, but nevertheless indispensable, Gospel of the Kingdom, many earnest Christians have jumped to the conclusion that the New Covenant is a covenant of personal salvation.

Our investigation of the actual terms of this covenant has, however, shown us that this cannot possibly be the case, because the New Covenant in Christ Jesus is a national covenant made with Israel and Judah and, moreover, one which is not yet in full operation.

The Promises made to the Fathers

The Gospel of Personal Salvation is an integral part, not of the New Covenant, but of the Abrahamic Covenant.

Under the Abrahamic Covenant the Seed of Abraham (that is to say, his lineal descendants) were to become a blessing to all the families of the earth; and the One Seed, the Messiah, was to become the greatest seed, and therefore the greatest blessing to all mankind.

The Abrahamic Covenant was, of course, made with the fathers of the Israel race, Abraham, Isaac and Israel; and it depended, not upon any condition, but solely upon the promises of God. For these reasons it is often described in the New Testament as the "Promises made to the Fathers."

Jesus came, as St. Paul tells us, to confirm the Promises made to the Fathers, in order that, by so doing, He might cause the Gentiles to glorify God for His mercy.

Thus the Messiah confirmed the Abrahamic Covenant in two ways: nationally, by introducing the New Covenant with Israel and Judah; and individually, by becoming the Saviour of the whole world.

Read Romans xv, 8-12; Galatians iii, 13-14.

The Atonement

In order to understand, however feebly, the mystery of the Great At-one-ment, or reconciliation of God with man, we must go back in mind to the very beginning of the Bible.

The Second Covenant, that which was made with Adam after the Fall, contains the first mention of the Saviour of the world, as the seed of the woman who should bruise the serpent's head. Just as, in the Abrahamic Covenant, He is the One Seed, or greatest seed, of Abraham, so in this Adamic Covenant, He is the One Seed, or greatest seed, of the human race.

Adam's sin was voluntary submission to Evil; and the wages of sin is death. By his trangression he brought physical and spiritual death, not only upon himself, but upon all his posterity.

The Love of God

The question is sometimes asked whether God, by a simple act of forgiveness, could not have excused Adam and Eve from the consequences of their folly. The fact of the Atonement proves that He could not.

God is a God of righteousness, the source of right, as

opposed to wrong; the source of order, as opposed to chaos; the source of law, as opposed to anarchy; the source of good, as opposed to evil.

The laws under which He established the universe are eternal and immutable; laws which may be described as an expression of His very being. It would have been inconsistent and illogical for the Creator to reverse those laws because man had transgressed them; only by changing His very nature could God have given to man a charter of immunity from the consequences of his own action.

If the matter had ended there, the Bible need not have been written. But God is also a God of love; not only a God actuated by love, but the source and fountain of love itself.

He could not reverse His laws, but He could, by divesting Himself of His divine powers and clothing Himself in human flesh, take the place of Adam, man for man; He could submit Himself to the temptation of Satan; He could take upon Himself the accumulated sins of all mankind, past, present and future, and suffer the inevitable consequence—death physical and spiritual.

This is the very core and centre of God's Great Plan of Salvation. For God so loved the world, that He gave His only-begotten Son, that whosoever believeth on Him should not perish, but have everlasting life.

Read John iii, 14-21.

The Rending of the Veil

At the moment of His death Jesus cried with a loud voice: "It is finished." He had completed the work which He came to do; the rest was in the hands of the Father. At the same instant the great curtain, or veil, of the Temple, which divided the Holy of Holies from the Holy Place, was torn from top to bottom by an unseen hand.

Read John xix, 30; Mark xv, 37-38.

The only way into the Holy of Holies was through the great veil, and hitherto only the High Priest had been allowed to use this way when he entered to make atonement for the sins of the people.

When Jesus had made the great and final atonement, the veil of the Temple was torn apart, and the Holy of Holies was laid bare to the gaze of all who stood by.

This dramatic event signified that, from the moment of His death, no priest was necessary to mediate between God and man, because Jesus Himself had become the Great High Priest, the only Mediator between God and man, and the only Way to the Father.

Read Hebrews vii, 24-28; ix, 1-15; ix, 24-28; x, 1-25; John xiv, 1-6.

The End of the Ordinances

By thus fulfilling the Law, Jesus brought to an end, not the whole of the Law of the Lord, as given to Israel through Moses, but only that part of it which was contained in the ordinances of divine worship.

In other words, He brought to an end those things which were typical of Himself as the Anointed Priest.

He ended the ordinances of the Law and substituted the Christian religion.

He ended the sacrifices and became Himself the "Lamb of God, which taketh away the sins of the world."

He ended the Aaronic priesthood and became Himself the Great High Priest.

He ended the veil of the Temple and became Himself the only Way of access to God the Father.

Read Ephesians ii, 15; 1 John ii, 1-7.

Chapter XXVII

THE DIVINITY OF THE MESSIAH

There are three main theories concerning the divinity of the Messiah which must be examined briefly in order to gain a proper understanding of a doctrine upon which so much of the Christian faith depends.

(1) The theory that Jesus of Nazareth was born of Joseph and Mary in the ordinary course of nature; that He had not been God before His birth, was not God during His life, and could not be God after His death.

We need not waste any time upon this view here, because the Bible asserts unequivocally that Jesus was born of a pure virgin by the "overshadowing" of God the Holy Spirit, and was therefore the only-begotten Son of God.

(2) The Kenosis Theory. This theory takes its name, which means "emptying," from a sentence in St. Paul's Epistle to the Philippians. The sentence is rendered in the Authorised Version: "(He) made Himself of no reputation"; but a more correct and literal translation, as given in the Revised Version, is "(He) emptied Himself."

Starting from this point, the advocates of the Kenosis Theory argue that Jesus, having emptied Himself of all His divine attributes, powers and prerogatives, was purely and simply a man like other men, and therefore liable to err in His claims and in His teaching.

The adoption of this theory leads to a mistrust of His teaching, disbelief in His miracles, denial of His divine origin, and in extreme cases, to the adoption of theory No. (1).

(3) The third theory is one which claims that Jesus, although born of woman, nevertheless retained during His mortal life all the nature, powers and attributes of God.

This theory, which is held by many earnest Christians, undoubtedly seeks to pay the highest honour to God the Son incarnate. But, paradoxically enough, it belittles the splendour of the sacrifice which He made in taking our

118

flesh upon Him; it tarnishes the brightness of His faith in the Father; and it dims the glory of His victorious life and death.

The sincerest advocates of this theory are fully aware of the difficulties which it brings in its train, and they attempt to meet these difficulties by saying that, although Jesus actually retained His divine powers, He never used them, except in certain circumstances.

This statement is, however, in direct conflict with the teaching of God the Son Himself. Nothing could be more emphatic than the assertions of Jesus on this very point. "The Son can do nothing of Himself, but what He seeth the Father do." "I can of Mine own self do nothing." "Then shall ye know that I am He, and that I do nothing of Myself."

Read John v, 19; v, 30; viii, 28.

We are forced, then, to the conclusion that this theory is both unscriptural and logically untenable. For if we admit that Jesus retained His divine powers during His mortal life, we must also admit the following corollaries:

(a) He could not have put Himself on trial in place of Adam, as man for man;

(b) He could not have proved that it was possible for man to live a sinless life;

(c) He could not have been put to death;

(d) He could not have demonstrated that it was possible for man to rise from the dead to everlasting life.

The Identity Theory

Where, then, are we to look for the truth concerning this all-important subject? Let us turn once more to that passage which has been so grossly misinterpreted by the advocates of the Kenosis Theory, making use of the more literal Revised Version.

Read Philippians ii, 5-11.

Before the dawn of time Jesus was the Second Person of the Trinity, God the Son, with all the inherent powers of the Godhead; and when time has ceased to be, He will

119

remain the same. But during the thirty-three and a half years of His mortal life He voluntarily emptied Himself, stripped Himself, or divested Himself, of those divine powers in order that He might carry out God's Great Plan of Salvation.

He willingly surrendered all His divine powers and became truly man. But there was one thing which He never surrendered, and which He retained throughout—His individuality, or identity, as the Second Person of the Trinity, God the Son.

If this thought be found difficult to assimilate, let us take as an illustration, but not as a parallel, the action of a king who abdicates his throne. Such a king empties himself, or divests himself, of all his royal powers, attributes, and prerogatives, and goes out into the world as an ordinary man. But nothing can take from him his identity as the son of his father.

Thus Jesus, having laid aside His divine powers, retained only His identity as God the Son; and this identity He clothed in the flesh of fallen humanity, taking upon Himself the mortal body which mankind possessed after the Fall, and referring to Himself, in the third person, as the Son of Man.

Read Romans viii, 3-4.

Life in Himself

Among those powers which Jesus surrendered was that quality which is called in the Bible "Life-in-Himself"; that is to say, not life by divine permission, but life by inherent right.

God alone has Life-in-Himself; He is Life; Death has no dominion over Him. It was therefore absolutely necessary that Jesus should empty Himself of this power in order that He might become "obedient unto death," and give His life a ransom for many.

Read Hebrews ii, 6-18.

Thus Jesus could say, referring to His immortal state, "As the Father hath Life-in-Himself, so hath He given to the Son to have Life-in-Himself"; and on the night before His crucifixion He could pray for the restoration of those

120

powers, which He had enjoyed with the Father before the world was.

Read John v, 18-30; xvii, 1-5.

The Baptism of the Holy Spirit

Here we may anticipate an objection that Jesus, in healing the sick, cleansing the lepers, and even raising the dead, was using divine powers, which He must have retained.

It is true that Jesus did all these things, but the Apostles also healed the sick, and even raised the dead.

Read John xiv, 12-14; Acts iii, 1-10; ix, 36-42.

As we have already seen, Jesus never claimed that He performed His miracles by virtue of His own powers and, indeed, expressly denied it on more than one occasion. By what power, then, did He do these things?

Again He leaves us in no doubt. "The words that I say unto you, I speak not from Myself; but the Father, that dwelleth in Me, He doeth the works."

Read John xiv, 10.

Before Jesus began His three years' ministry, John the Baptist was preaching the Gospel of the Kingdom, and baptising on the banks of the Jordan. To the crowds who came to hear him, John made this statement: "I indeed baptise you with water; but there cometh One who is mightier than I. He shall baptise you with the Holy Ghost and with fire."

Jesus received from John the baptism of water. But as He came up out of the river the heavens were opened, the Holy Ghost descended upon Him in the form of a dove, and a voice came from Heaven, saying: "This is My beloved Son, in whom I am well pleased."

Read Matthew iii, 11-17.

In that tremendous moment Jesus received the baptism of the Holy Spirit, the baptism of fire. It was in the power of this baptism that He healed the sick; it was in the power of this baptism that He overcame temptation; it was in the power of this baptism that He led His perfect life.

Jesus set an example, an ideal, for all to follow; but He did not expect, and does not now expect, His disciples to

121

follow that example without the power which He Himself enjoyed. His last act upon this earth was to promise this great gift to His faithful Apostles: "John truly baptised you with water; but ye shall be baptised with the Holy Ghost not many days hence. Ye shall receive power, after that the Holy Ghost is come upon you."

Read Acts i, 1-9; ii, 1-21.

In the power of that baptism, which descended upon them at the Feast of Pentecost, the Apostles healed the sick; in the power of that baptism the Apostles raised the dead; in the power of that baptism the Apostles gave up their lives in His service.

That same baptism the Apostles were able to pass on to others by the laying on of hands. They baptised all their converts with water in the name of the Lord Jesus, but to some they gave the baptism of fire.

This baptism, the baptism of the Holy Spirit, the baptism of fire, the baptism of power, the Lord Jesus offers to-day to all who will prepare themselves to receive it.

Jesus Himself was thirty years old when He went to John to be baptised. After thirty years of perfect preparation He received the baptism of the Holy Spirit, not "by measure," but in its fullest capacity. He could therefore do what He did, not by virtue of His own power, but by virtue of His baptism.

Read John iii, 34-35.

The Athanasian Creed

The truth concerning the divinity of the Messiah is set forth once for all in that great statement of Christian doctrine which is called the Creed of Athanasius.

"For the right faith is that we believe, and confess, that our Lord Jesus Christ, the Son of God, is God and man.

"God, of the substance of the Father, begotten before the worlds; and man, of the substance of his mother, born in the world;

"Perfect God, and perfect man; of a reasonable soul and human flesh subsisting;

"Equal to the Father, as touching His Godhead; and inferior to the Father as touching His manhood.

122

"Who although He be God and man; yet He is not two, but one Christ;

"One; not by conversion of the Godhead into flesh; but by taking of the manhood into God;

"One altogether; not by confusion of substance; but by unity of Person.

"For as the reasonable soul and flesh is one man; so God and man is one Christ."

We cannot doubt, then, that the Godhead was not converted into flesh by the incarnation of God the Son. Jesus was truly man, divested for a little while of His divine powers, but nevertheless retaining His identity as the only-begotten Son of God.

CHAPTER XXVIII

THE SPIRITUAL-ISRAEL THEORY

Overwhelming proof of the identity of Jesus of Nazareth with the Messiah is afforded by His fulfilment of prophecy down to the least significant material details. Nevertheless, there was one complete set of prophecies which He failed to fulfil. We refer, of course, to the numerous prophecies concerning His kingship, and particularly to those which had been made through the mouths of the prophet Isaiah and of the archangel Gabriel.

Read Isaiah ix, 6-7; Luke i, 26-33.

Did Jesus take upon His shoulders the government of the world and usher in His reign of universal righteousness, and justice, and peace?

The history of the world for the last 1,900 years, and the columns of our own daily Press should be sufficient answer.

Did Jesus take the throne of His ancestor David and reign over the House of Israel?

The dynasty of David apparently came to an end with King Zedekiah in B.C. 587, and the House of Israel had been lost among the Gentiles.

Did He reign even over that small portion of Judah, called the Jews?

The Jews shouted: "We have no king but Cæsar. Away with Him! Crucify Him! His blood be upon us, and on our children!"

Was He a king?

To Pilate, who asked that very question, He acknowledged that He was by right a king, but He went on to say: "For this cause came I into the world, that I might bear witness unto the truth."

Read John xviii, 37.

The Great Witness

The truth to which Jesus bore witness was the truth of the Old Testament Scriptures, which showed that He must sacrifice His own life as the Anointed Priest, before He could take the throne of His ancestor David as the Anointed King.

Throughout His ministry Jesus pleaded with the Jews to listen to the truth. But they despised His teaching, and rejected His claims; they insisted upon putting Him to death, taking the guilt of His blood upon themselves. Powerless to interfere, Jesus could only weep over their self-imposed curse.

Read Luke xix, 41-44; Matthew xxiii, 34-38; xxvii, 22-25.

The Destruction of Jerusalem

Thirty-seven years after His death the prophetic words of Jesus were fulfilled to the letter. Titus, general of the armies of his father Vespasian, having marched into Palestine with 80,000 men to quell an insurrection, entrenched his forces around Jerusalem and starved the city into surrender.

Thousands of Judæans fell by the sword; thousands died of famine and disease; while the remainder were sold into slavery. Jerusalem was burnt down, and the magnificent temple, begun by Herod the Great in B.C. 17, and finished in A.D. 64, was razed to the ground.

The Mystery of the Kingdom

With the utter destruction of Jerusalem in A.D. 70, we

arrive at a point from which we can survey once more the development of God's Great Plan of Salvation.

In strict accordance with prophecy the Messiah has been born into the seed of Abraham, the race of Israel, the tribe of Judah, and the house of David. He has become the Redeemer of Israel and the Saviour of the world. He has sacrificed His own life, descended into Hell, risen from the dead, and ascended to the right hand of the Father.

All this has been accomplished. But what has become of that great nation which He redeemed on Calvary? What has become of the solemn covenant with Abraham, Isaac and Israel? What has become of the equally solemn covenant with David?

The Jews, the only visible part of the race of Israel, have been scattered by the Romans over the face of the earth. The greater part of the kingdom of Judah did not return from its captivity in Babylonia. The dynasty of David was apparently extinguished by the murder of the sons of King Zedekiah in B.C. 587. The ten tribes of the kingdom of Israel were lost in Media in B.C. 676.

These questions have been, and are still, a stumbling-block to many earnest students of the Bible.

Spiritual Israel

By way of answer, some theologians have propounded a theory in which they state that God found that His original plan would not work; that circumstances had so changed that it never could work; that in consequence He was obliged to break His Promises to Abraham, Isaac, Israel and David; and that, having broken those promises, He transferred all the blessings of the Israel covenants, but not the curses, to the Christian Church.

Under this theory it would seem that up to B.C. 676 Israel is to be taken as a literal nation; after that date it would appear that Israel becomes the Church, or the Church becomes what is known as "Spiritual Israel." In the same way, the throne of David is apparently to be regarded as a literal dynasty up to B.C. 587, and after that date as the spiritual throne of God the Son.

125

Chapter Headings

This theory, which is held by a great many earnest Christians, has undoubtedly been fostered by the chapter headings which are to be found in some editions of the Bible. It should, however, be understood that these headings form no part of the original text; on the contrary, they have been added by editors who believed sincerely, but mistakenly, that they were bridging a gap in God's Great Plan of Salvation which was otherwise impassable.

A Half Truth

Although this theory will not stand careful investigation, we must not make the mistake of dismissing it too lightly, because it does embody a certain portion of the truth.

As we have noted already, Gentile Christians do become part of Israel by adoption. But that very word "adoption" implies a family into which they may be adopted; a family of Israelites by race, whose privileges and responsibilities the Gentiles may share by grace.

While, therefore, it is true to say that the spiritual Church has become part of racial Israel, it is not true to say that racial Israel has been transformed into the spiritual Church.

Nor is it true to say that the throne or dynasty of David has already become the throne of God the Son. For if that throne, founded upon earth, has been transferred to heaven, why is an increase of justice and peace necessary in a sphere where the will of God already reigns supreme?

Even if it were possible to overcome these obstacles, if all the rest of the Old Testament could be spiritualised, it would still be necessary to explain the stubborn fact of the Jews, who remain to this day a standing proof, not only of the spiritual, but also of the material truth of the Bible.

Faith Undermined

Thus when we try to apply the Spiritual Israel Theory to our studies, we find ourselves beset by so many difficulties, contradictions and absurdities, that we must adopt one of two courses. We must either reject it altogether or, if we feel compelled to accept it, we must at the same time reject the greater part of the book on which our faith is founded.

If we adopt the latter alternative we are immediately faced by a terrible dilemma. If God has broken His oath to Abraham, Isaac and Israel; if He has broken His oath to David; if He has broken any one promise which He ever made, how can we be sure that He will not break His promise again? How can we trust God to keep His promise of everlasting life to those who believe in His Son?

Obviously, then, if we admit into our minds any doubt whatsoever as to the power, or the will, of God to keep His promises, we immediately begin to undermine the very foundations on which the Christian faith is built up.

The Epistle to the Hebrews states that God confirmed His promise to Abraham by an oath, because He wished to show to the heirs of the covenant the "immutability of His counsel"; and it describes the promise and the oath as "two immutable things, in which it was impossible for God to lie."

The Spiritual Israel Theory states that it was possible for God to lie and to break both His promise and His oath.

True Christians will hesitate to blaspheme God by accusing Him of perjury; they will find that the whole Bible is opposed to this theory, that the New Testament flatly contradicts it, while the Book of Jeremiah exposes its falsity.

Read Hebrews vi, 11-20; Jeremiah xxxiii, 23-26.

CHAPTER XXIX

THE WISDOM OF THE SIMPLE

It should now be possible for us to continue our studies in the certain assurance that all the unconditional covenants still wait for complete fulfilment, because they depend upon the honour of a Supreme Being who, by His very nature, cannot change His mind or break His word.

The finite mind finds it difficult to understand that God stands outside the limitations of time, and can therefore see the end from the beginning. It is, perhaps, even more difficult to grasp the fact that God can endow man with free will, and yet reveal beforehand exactly what use man will make of this great gift.

Read Isaiah xlvi, 9-10.

The Light of the World

Nevertheless we have seen already how exactly, and with what a wealth of detail, God revealed beforehand the circumstances of the birth, life, death and resurrection of the Messiah.

Is it unreasonable, then, to suppose that God may have given some indication of the manner in which He will be faithful to His other promises?

God the Son came into this world to bear witness to the Truth. He claimed that He was the Truth, the Light of the World, the Living Word of God.

It is to Jesus, therefore, that we must look for the light which will lead us to the truth. But we must go to Him in humbleness and faith; we must clear our minds of preconceived ideas and prejudices; we must even be prepared to sacrifice our most cherished theories if need be. We must, in fact, listen to His words as little children, ready and willing to be taught; for we have His warning that, unless we do this, our quest will be in vain.

Read Matthew xviii, 1-6.

By making this surrender in all meekness and lowliness of heart, we take His yoke upon us; by taking His yoke upon us, we learn of Him; by learning of Him, we acquire the understanding of the simple. We acquire that wisdom which is greater than knowledge, and which springs from reverence for "every word that proceedeth out of the mouth of God."

Read Matthew xi, 28-30; Psalm xix, 7; cxi, 10; Matthew iv, 3-4.

The Apostles went to Jesus with the simple faith of little children, and to them He said: "Unto you it is given to know the mysteries of the Kingdom of God; but to others in parables." Those who were wise and prudent in their own eyes also went to Him, and came away unenlightened.

Read Luke viii, 9-10; x, 21-24.

When we ourselves go to Jesus in this spirit, He meets us with the ringing command: "Search the Scriptures; for these are they which testify of Me." And when, like children, we ask: "What are the Scriptures?" we hear His reply: "The writings of Moses, the writings of the Prophets, and the Psalms."

Read John v, 39-47; Luke xxiv, 25-27; xxiv, 44-45.

If, then, we have sufficient faith to believe every word which Jesus uttered, whether we can explain it or not, we must search the Old Testament as well as the New; and we shall do so in the certain assurance that, if the Author and Finisher of our faith could open the minds of His Apostles to the truths of the Scriptures, He will open our understanding also, provided we go to Him in the same spirit.

CHAPTER XXX

THE APPOINTED PLACE

The difficulty which still confronts us is that which arises from the announcement made by the Archangel Gabriel to the Virgin Mary: "The Lord God shall give unto Him the throne of His father David; and He shall reign over the House of Jacob for ever." For if the dynasty of David and the House of Israel have finally ceased to exist, this prophecy can never be fulfilled.

We must, then, put to ourselves this question: "Has God revealed in His Holy Scriptures how, and in what manner, He will fulfil the remainder of His promises?"

The Davidic Covenant

When we turn back to the institution of the dynasty of David, we find that David was very anxious to build a temple for the Lord in Jerusalem; but the word of the Lord came to him by the mouth of the prophet Nathan to say that this great privilege had been reserved for his son.

David was not to be allowed to build a house (temple)

for God; but God Himself would build a house (dynasty) for David. This dynasty was to be over the kingdom of Israel, and both throne and kingdom were to endure for ever.

One particular clause in this covenant may have sounded strangely in the ears of Nathan and David, for Israel was at that time firmly planted in the Promised Land in accordance with the Abrahamic Covenant. But God, who sees the end from the beginning, knew the punishment which the House of David and the People of Israel would bring upon themselves in after days; He knew that they must be uprooted from the Promised Land in accordance with the Mosaic Covenant, and for this reason He embodied in His covenant with David a special promise which should reveal to future generations how He would keep His word, in spite of human incredulity and opposition.

"I will appoint a place for My people, Israel, and will plant them, that they may dwell in a place of their own, and move no more; neither shall the children of wickedness afflict them any more, as beforetime."

Read 2 Samuel vii, 10.

The Faithfulness of God

Troublous times fell upon the whole people of Israel when they forsook the Law of the Lord. After the kingdom had been divided, disaster followed upon disaster, until eventually both Israel and Judah were uprooted from the Promised Land.

Yet throughout all this period of national failure we find God asserting in the most emphatic terms that He will be faithful to His covenants, and scorning the very idea that He can break His sacred word.

Read Isaiah lv, 8-11; Jeremiah xxiii, 3-8; xxxi, 35-37; xxxiii, 14-26.

The gathering of the scattered tribes into the Appointed Place is vividly foretold in Psalm cvii, where Israel is described as the "Redeemed of the Lord," and the Appointed place as the "city of habitation."

Read Psalm cvii.

Further search leads us to other passages which describe the gathering of Israel into the Appointed Place.

Read Ezekiel xxviii, 25-26; xxxvi, 16-24.

Israel's Future Predicted

Having progressed so far, we find that the tribes of Israel are to be scattered among the Gentiles, losing their name, but preserving their distinctive nationality; they are to lead a nomadic life, travelling by routes which are unknown to them; they are to be shepherded like flocks of sheep into the Appointed Place.

In the Appointed Place they are to increase and multiply exceedingly; they are to find the confines of their new home too narrow for them; they are to spread abroad to the west, and to the east, and to the north, and to the south; they are to lose their first colony, but expand into a nation and commonwealth of nations.

During this period they are to become a Christian nation, witnesses to the truth of God, and missionaries of His Holy Word; they are to be a maritime and a colonising nation; they are to free the slaves, to relieve oppression, and to administer justice.

Eventually their identity is to be revealed to themselves and to the world; the capital of this nation and commonwealth of nations is to be transferred to Jerusalem; and a representative portion of the Israel people is to be regathered into the Promised Land.

Islands

In the prophecies which reveal the gathering and regathering of Israel, the Appointed Place is repeatedly described as "islands."

The first passages which we will consider describe the regathering of Israel and Judah as being from the "islands of the sea."

Read Isaiah xi, 11-13; xxiv, 15-16.

In the next passage Israel in the isles is exhorted to rest and recuperate in the certain assurance of the faithfulness of God.

Read Isaiah xli, 1-10.

Isles at the End of the Earth

Passing on to the next chapter we find the islands described as being at the end of the earth which, of course, means the end of the earth as it was known in ancient times.

Here the prophet visualises Israel as a maritime nation, waiting for the Second Advent of the Messiah to take His throne as her everlasting King; and commissions her to give the whole Gospel of God to the Gentiles, to relieve oppression, and to free slaves.

Read Isaiah xlii, 1-13.

The last part of the chapter describes how the Israelites are led, like blind men, by unknown ways into the Appointed Place; and emphasises their prolonged ignorance as to their real identity.

Read Isaiah xlii, 16-20.

Isles afar off in the North-west

Continuing our studies, we now find the islands described as being far off from the Holy Land, and to the north-west of it. The Hebrew language contains no single term for "north-west"; this direction is therefore conveyed by the expression "north and west."

Israel now becomes a great colonising nation, and is again commissioned to free the slaves and to take the Gospel to the Gentiles.

Read Isaiah xlix, 1-12.

Later in the same chapter we find that Israel loses her first colony and, being unable to contain her increasing population, acquires more colonies.

Read Isaiah xlix, 13-21; Genesis xxviii, 13-15; xxxv, 9-12.

In chapter li we are again shown the vision of Israel in the isles waiting for the return of her Redeemer to reign over her as King.

Read Isaiah li, 1-5.

Isles Afar Off

Turning next to the prophet Jeremiah, we find that the regathering of Israel and Judah is to be selective, "one of a city and two of a family." This representative body is to

132

be brought back to the Holy Land out of "the land of the north," and from the "isles afar off."

Read Jeremiah iii, 12-23; xxxi, 1-11.

Preservation of the Throne of David

Bearing in mind that the promise of the Appointed Place is only one clause in the Davidic Covenant, we may reasonably expect some revelation as to the manner in which God would fulfil the remaining clauses.

It will be remembered that this covenant imposed no conditions, and was not dependent upon the conduct of either David or his successors for final fulfilment. At the same time it did provide for the correction and punishment of the reigning princes of the royal line for any failure to live up to their high calling.

Read Psalm lxxxix, 18-37.

As a result of his departure from the Law of the Lord, Solomon was responsible for the loss of the ten tribes of Israel; and his successors, with one or two exceptions, brought disaster after disaster upon themselves and upon their country.

Nevertheless, nearly 500 years after the making of the covenant, when the House of David was rushing headlong to its downfall, we find the Lord God repudiating with divine scorn the very suggestion that He could be faithless to His promises.

Read Jeremiah xxxiii, 17-26.

In B.C. 587 the dynasty of David came to an apparent end when Zedekiah was compelled to witness the murder of his sons before his own eyes were put out.

Zedekiah's daughters, however, escaped assassination, possibly because they had been hidden, or possibly because Nebuchadnezzar did not know that the female sex was no bar to succession under Israel law. But these princesses were not destined to remain in Palestine for, after the departure of the Chaldæan armies, certain Judahites who had escaped deportation, fled to Egypt, and forced the king's daughters, together with Jeremiah the prophet and Baruch the scribe, to accompany them.

Read Jeremiah xliii, 1-7.

At Tahpanhes the history of Zedekiah's daughters comes to an end so far as the Bible is concerned. But history pre-written, which is prophecy, has something more to say about the princess who should save the royal dynasty of David from extinction.

The Parable of the Cedar

The revelation comes to us in the form of a parable which was spoken by the mouth of the Lord to the prophet Ezekiel.

Read Ezekiel xvii, 1-10.

From the interpretation which follows, it is clear that the cedar stands for the royal house of David. The first eagle (king Nebuchadnezzar of Babylon) had taken the highest branch (Jehoiachim), and his young twigs (Jehoiachin and other princes), captive to a city of merchants (Babylon).

Nebuchadnezzar had then made a covenant, or treaty, with Jehoiachim's brother, Zedekiah, and set him up on the throne of Judah as a vassal of Babylon. But Zedekiah had broken the treaty with Babylon and allied himself with the second eagle, Egypt.

For this perfidy it is decreed that Zedekiah shall be cast down from the throne and taken to Babylon, while his kingdom is scattered to the winds.

Read Ezekiel xvii, 11-21.

The Tender Twig

For that part of the parable which immediately concerns us, no explanation is given. But the interpretation of the first part of the parable makes it clear that the Lord God is stating that He will take one of the young twigs (children) of the highest branch of the cedar (Zedekiah), and plant it in another place, where it shall take root and grow into another great cedar (royal house).

When we call to mind the divine commission of the prophet Jeremiah, we are led still nearer to the interpretation of this parable. That commission reads: "See I have this day set thee over the nations, and over the kingdoms, to root out, and to pull down, and to destroy, and to throw down, to build and to plant."

Read Jeremiah i, 10.

In superintending the rooting out and the pulling down of the dynasty of David, Jeremiah carried out the first part of his commission; it remained for him to build and to plant. He could not take any of the sons of Zedekiah because they had been murdered; therefore he took a tender twig, a daughter, and carried her off to Egypt.

We cannot, however, imagine that he planted the tender twig in Egypt. Unless the purposes of God have been defeated by puny man, this princess was planted by Jeremiah in the mountain (kingdom) of the height of Israel; that is to say, in the Appointed Place, the isles of the north-west.

Read Jeremiah xxxi, 27-28; Ezekiel xvii, 22-24.

Israel's Destiny

To sum up, then, Israel's Appointed Place consists of a group of islands lying to the north-west of Palestine, and so far off as to be in the uttermost part of the ancient world.

Settled in these islands, Israel is to be a maritime and colonising nation, expanding west, east, north and south, in that exact order.

She is to lose her first colony, and then acquire others, thus cultivating the waste spaces of the earth, relieving oppression, and freeing the slaves.

During this period of expansion she is to be a Christian nation, taking the whole Gospel of God to the ends of the world.

In course of time she is to become a nation and a company of nations; that is to say, an empire.

Finally, the throne of Israel in the isles is to be occupied by a prince of the House of David until He shall come whose right it is to rule, great David's greater Son, the Everlasting King.

Chapter XXXI

THE STONE OF ISRAEL

It will be remembered that Jacob, fleeing from the wrath of his twin brother Esau, came at nightfall to a lonely place, where he lay down to sleep, taking one of the stones of the place for a pillow.

While asleep he had a marvellous dream or vision, in which God repeated to him the covenant which He had already made with his father Isaac, and with his grandfather Abraham.

The vision was so vivid and so real that in the morning Jacob named the place Beth-el (House of God), and consecrated the stone which he had used for a pillow by pouring oil upon it and making a vow of self-dedication. This was a very solemn act. There was no witness to the covenant which had just been made between God and himself; therefore he consecrated the stone on which his head had rested, and made it, as it were, the title-deed to his inheritance.

That he regarded the stone as a symbol of the future greatness of his house, is evident from his words, "And this stone, which I have set for a pillar, shall be God's house" (Beth-el).

Read Genesis xxviii.

Twenty years later God commanded Jacob to return to his native land, and referred to Himself as the "God of Beth-el, where thou anointedst the pillar," thus setting the seal of His divine authority upon the stone as the witness of the covenant.

Read Genesis xxxi, 13.

After his return Jacob was commanded to go again to Beth-el, where he had left the stone.

Read Genesis xxxv, 1.

There God confirmed the previous vision, and changed Jacob's name to Israel (Ruling with God); while Jacob re-consecrated the stone by pouring wine and oil upon it.

Read Genesis xxxv, 9-15.

From that time forward the stone undoubtedly became a treasured possession, for we find Israel referring to it on his death-bed in Egypt, when he seems to have placed it in the custody of Joseph, together with the birthright.

Read Genesis xlix, 22-26.

After the exodus from Egypt we find Joshua setting it up outside the Tabernacle of the Lord, and calling it a stone of witness, which "hath heard all the words of the Lord."

Read Joshua xxiv, 26-27.

Later still, the stone of Israel was set up in the Temple of Solomon. Kings were crowned either sitting upon it or standing by it, and it was also used for royal proclamations.

Read 2 Kings xi, 12-14; xxiii, 1-3.

Thus the Kingdom of God on earth became known as the Kingdom of the Stone, because that stone was the sole witness to the covenant which God had made with Jacob-Israel on two separate occasions.

CHAPTER XXXII

THE KINGDOM OF THE STONE

If the purpose of the Bible is to reveal the character of God and His purposes for mankind, then the whole book may be said to be prophetic.

The word "prophet" is derived from a Greek word which means "one who speaks on behalf of another." The prophets of God in the Bible were therefore men and women to whom God spoke, and who, in their turn, spoke for God to the world.

Abraham, Isaac, Israel, Joseph, Moses, Joshua, David, Elijah, Isaiah, Jeremiah, and Ezekiel, to mention only a few, were all prophets in the strict sense of the word. John the Baptist was described by Jesus as the greatest prophet of all; John, Peter, Paul, and the other Apostles, were prophets; while our Lord Himself stands alone as the Living Word of God.

Prophecy

Prediction of the future was not an essential part of prophecy; the prophets were chosen to receive the words of God and to transmit them to their fellow-men. Nevertheless, God did from time to time reveal certain portions of His purposes, in order that the fulfilment of these purposes might justify and strengthen the faith of man.

Inspiration

Men of widely different character, living at different times and in different places, "spake as they were moved by the Holy Ghost"; and each one revealed some particular phase of one harmonious whole. Thus prophecy, so far from being a matter of individual prediction, came through all its human channels from one source, and one source only, God the Holy Spirit.

The inspiration and continuity of prophecy from the earliest times were abundantly confirmed, "made more sure," by our Lord, who stated that He Himself came to fulfil the Law and the Prophets. We shall therefore be following in His footsteps if we make use of prophecy as a "light that shineth in a dark place."

Read Hebrews i, 1-2; 2 Timothy iii, 14-17; 2 Peter i, 19-21.

Daniel

To co-ordinate the various phases of prophetic revelation, we need what may be called a "key" prophecy; and this is supplied to us by Daniel, whose authenticity as a prophet is guaranteed by the greatest Prophet of all time.

Read Matthew xxiv, 15.

Daniel, according to Josephus the historian, was a prince of the royal House of David. As a young man he was carried captive to Babylon in B.C. 606, nineteen years before the destruction of Jerusalem by king Nebuchadnezzar in B.C. 587.

After his arrival in Babylon, he was taken into the service of the king under the name of Belteshazzar, and lodged in the royal palace together with three other young men, Hananiah, Mishael and Azariah, whose names were changed

138

to Shadrach, Meshach and Abed-nego, and who were afterwards delivered miraculously from the midst of the burning fiery furnace.

Read Daniel i, 1-7.

As time went on, Daniel and his three companions, young as they were, acquired a great reputation for learning and wisdom, and the king trusted them more than all the magicians and astrologers in his realm.

Read Daniel i, 17-21.

Nebuchadnezzar's Dream

In the year B.C. 602 an extraordinary thing happened, for the king dreamt a dream which he promptly forgot. But the memory of the dream troubled him so much that he could not sleep at night.

Worried as he was, he called together all the wise men of his empire, Daniel and his three companions among them, and commanded them, under pain of violent death, to recount to him the dream. The command was utterly unreasonable, as the astrologers pointed out, but the king was an absolute autocrat, and he meant what he said. The Chaldæans therefore prepared for death, but Daniel and his companions prayed to the Lord for help.

Read Daniel ii, 1-18.

That same night both the dream and the interpretation of it were revealed to Daniel, who repeated them to the king.

Read Daniel ii, 19-49.

The Interpretation

The figure of the image in the dream represented four great empires, diverse in character, and yet all part of the same system; four great empires, which were to appear, not simultaneously, but in succession.

Identification of these empires is made easy by Daniel's words to Nebuchadnezzar: "Thou art this head of gold." The first empire, then, was Babylon; the second empire, portrayed by the breast and arms of silver, Medo-Persia;

the third empire, portrayed by the belly and thighs of brass, Greece; the fourth empire, portrayed by the legs of iron, Rome, which was to divide into two parts and develop into the kingdoms and republics portrayed by the feet, partly iron and partly clay.

At this point a fifth empire appears, which has been in process of development under the four empires, but is not part of the system to which they belong, and is not destined to have a successor. After pulverising the remnants of the fourth empire, and obliterating the whole image, this empire expands until it fills the whole earth.

So far we have been travelling down the stream of time in the region of prophecy fulfilled, which is history; now we are approaching the region of history foretold, which is prophecy. We have traced the rise and fall of the Babylonian, Medo-Persian, Greek, and Roman Empires; and we know that another empire has already arisen, the like of which has never been seen before.

The Babylonian System

The metal figure of the image in the dream represents the rebellious usurpation by man of divine authority in political government. In other words, the various governments under this system were to be, and have been up tp this day, political entities carved out by the hand of man, but nevertheless permitted by God to continue for a certain length of time, in order that every system of government, except the divine system, might be tried and proved a failure.

For this condition of affairs the Kingdom of the Stone was largely responsible. The divine system had been entrusted to her for demonstration to the world, but she had been false to her trust, and for that failure had been scattered among the nations. While still lost, she is redeemed and restored. And when, in due course, the four empires of the Babylonian succession have passed away, the Kingdom of the Stone reappears as the fifth empire, charged with the commission of establishing the divine system in place of that system which takes its name from the place of its birth, Babylon.

Read Isaiah xli, 14-16; Revelation xviii.

140

Divine Origin of the Stone Kingdom

In the dream the fifth empire is represented as a stone "cut out of the mountain without hands," and we cannot help asking ourselves the question: "Cut out of what mountain, and by what agency?"

The answer is given to us by God Himself through the mouth of the prophet Isaiah.

"Hearken to me, ye that follow after righteousness, ye that seek the Lord, look unto the rock whence ye are hewn, and to the hole of the pit whence ye are digged.

"Look unto Abraham your father, and unto Sarah that bare you; for I called him alone, and blessed him, and increased him."

Read Isaiah li, 1-2.

Abraham and Sarah, the great progenitors of the Israel people, were cut out from the corrupt civilisation of their time, not by the hand of man, but by the will of God. They were called out of Ur of the Chaldees by the word of the Lord Himself, in order that they might be the founders of a great nation, which should be a blessing to all the families of the earth.

Read Genesis xii, 1-3.

It is clear, then, that the "Stone cut out without hands" represents, not a political entity carved out by man for himself, but a nation created by the will of God; a nation, moreover, specially developed into an empire, and endowed with greatness, not for the gratification of its own selfish ambitions, but for the express purpose of being a blessing to all the families of the earth.

The Mountain Empire

That brings us up to our own times. But the vision does not end there, for the stone was to grow into a mountain so large that it filled the whole world. Where shall we find an explanation of this phenomenon? Let us turn again to the prophet Isaiah.

"And it shall come to pass in the last days, that the mountain of the Lord's house shall be established in the top of the mountains, and shall be exalted above the hills; and all nations shall flow into it.

"And many people shall go and say, Come ye, and let us go up to the mountain of the Lord, to the house of the God of Jacob; and He will teach us of His ways, and we will walk in His paths; for out of Zion shall go forth the Law, and the word of the Lord from Jerusalem."

Read Isaiah ii, 1-5.

The Stone Kingdom of Israel has already grown into the Mountain Empire of Britain; so much is history. From this point we look forward into the future, and we see the nations of the world coming joyfully into the Mountains of the Lord's House, under the direct rule of Jesus Christ the King.

Thus the vision of St. John becomes at length a glorious reality, and all the kingdoms of this world become the Kingdom of our Lord and of His Christ, who shall reign for ever and ever.

Read Revelation xi, 15.

The Kingdom of God

With these thoughts in our minds we can realise more fully the significance of our Lord's statement on the very day of His death.

"My kingdom is not of this world; if My kingdom were of this world, then would My servants fight, that I should not be delivered to the Jews; but now is My kingdom not from hence."

Standing face to face with Pontius Pilate, the Roman governor of Judæa, Jesus was addressing the representative of the fourth empire of the Babylonian succession; and He was, in effect, telling him that His Kingdom was not part of the existing world system, or Babylonian succession.

Read John xviii, 33-36.

The Kingdom of Jesus Christ is the Kingdom of the Stone cut out without hands, a servant nation specially created by God to carry out His purposes in the earth. Already the Kingdom of the Stone has developed into an empire, and the Babylonian succession has all but finished its course.

When our Lord returns and takes His rightful place on the throne, His Kingdom will draw unto itself all the kingdoms, nations and peoples of the whole world.

Chapter XXXIII

THE RESPONSIBILITY OF ISRAEL

To this Israel afar off in the islands of the north-west, to the only empire consisting of a nation and a commonwealth of free nations which the world has ever seen, to this people whose kings are still crowned on the traditional stone of Israel, comes the command of the Everlasting King: "Occupy till I come."

Read Luke xix, 11-27; Matthew xxv, 14-46; Mark xiii, 32-37.

From a study of the parable of the nobleman who went into a far country, as it occurs in the first three Gospels, we gather that the time of its utterance was only a few days before the crucifixion. Jesus was about to make His triumphal entry into Jerusalem amid the plaudits of the people and the shouts of "Hosanna! Blessed is the King of Israel that cometh in the name of the Lord"; the people were expecting Him to declare Himself as King, "because He was nigh to Jerusalem, and because they thought that the Kingdom of God should immediately appear."

A National Parable

Although many valuable personal lessons may be learnt from this parable, its prime significance is clearly national; and its interpretation, from this point of view, presents little difficulty.

The nobleman is, of course, our Lord Himself, who was about "to leave this world, and to sit down at the right hand of the Majesty on High, until the time should come for Him to return as King. The citizens, who hated him, are obviously the Judæans, whose hatred was so intense that they put Him to the death of the cross; and it is worth noting that the citizens sent a message to the nobleman,

143

after he had left them, saying: 'We will not have this man to reign over us'; a parallel which exactly describes the attitude of the Jews to Jesus from that day to this."

No pounds were given to the citizens, because the kingdom had been taken from the Jews and given to a nation which should bring forth the fruits of the kingdom. That nation, the ten-tribed kingdom of Israel, is portrayed in St. Luke's version as the ten servants who received ten pounds, and in St. Matthew's version as the servants to whom the nobleman delivered his goods. Neither version gives an exact description of the goods, and for this we must turn to St. Paul.

Read Romans ix, 3-5.

The rest of the parable describes the actions of the nobleman immediately after his return as king. He reckons first with the ten servants, and then with the citizens.

St. Mark's very brief version of the parable leaves us in no doubt as to what is meant by the return of the nobleman, and St. Matthew's version continues with the following words.

"When the Son of Man shall come in His glory, and all the holy angels with Him, then shall He sit upon the throne of His glory;

"And before Him shall be gathered all nations; and He shall separate them one from another, as a shepherd divideth his sheep from the goats."

So the reckoning is with nations; with Israel and Judah first, then with all the other nations of the world.

The Talents and the Pounds

Once again, then, Israel has been entrusted with a glorious privilege and a terrible responsibility; for during the absence of her Lord and Master all the treasures of the Kingdom of God have been given into her keeping, with the command: "Occupy till I come."

The Throne of the Lord over Israel, the Kingdom of God on earth, the Law of the Lord, and the truth of the sacred Scriptures, all these Israel must maintain, without loss and with profit, until the greatest Nobleman of all time returns from the far country to claim those precious things which belong to Him alone.

CHAPTER XXXIV

THE SEED OF ABRAHAM

Before Jesus began His short ministry of three years, His cousin John the Baptist was preaching the Gospel of the Kingdom and announcing the imminent coming of the Messiah.

His converts came probably, in the main, from the common people, who were downtrodden and oppressed alike by their Roman conquerors and by their own national leaders. They rejoiced in the advent of the long-expected Messiah, and were anxious to prepare themselves for His coming.

When, however, John "saw many of the Pharisees and Sadducees come to his baptism, he said unto them, O generation of vipers, who hath warned *you* to flee from the wrath to come?"

Read Matthew iii, 1-12.

Harsh words these, to men who had come to his baptism; and yet not so harsh as those which, in after days, were addressed to the scribes and Pharisees by the Messiah Himself.

"Woe unto you, scribes and Pharisees, hypocrites! For ye shut up the kingdom of heaven against men; for ye neither go in yourself, neither suffer ye them that are entering to go in.

"Ye serpents, ye generation of vipers, how can ye escape the damnation of hell?"

Read Matthew xxiii, 13-39.

Why, then, did these men come out to John at all? Certainly not in any spirit of repentance; that is made clear by John's next remark: "Bring forth therefore fruits meet for repentance."

As leaders of Jewish thought they were probably seeking information as to this new revival, appraising its value, and speculating as to its development. They felt in themselves no need for repentance or reform because they based all their hopes of salvation upon their nationality.

They misunderstood the nature and purpose of the Abrahamic Covenant as completely as do many people to-day. Indeed, at a later date, we find them carrying on a bitter controversy on this very point with our Lord Himself.

Read John viii, 31-59.

National and Individual Salvation

The Abrahamic Covenant was, of course, national in character. In selecting Abraham, Isaac and Jacob, the great progenitors of the Children of Israel, God was laying the foundations of a great nation and kingdom, which should be His instrument for delivering the message of His Great Plan of Salvation to all mankind.

In order that it might achieve the purpose for which it had been created, God promised to this kingdom national salvation; but He did not promise, or even imply, unconditional spiritual salvation for the individuals who should, from time to time, compose that kingdom.

The nation of Israel has endured throughout the ages, and will continue to endure; but the individual members of the nation do not endure, at least not on the terrestrial plane. In the natural course of events their bodies perish, and their spiritual salvation is a personal matter between themselves and their Maker.

At the same time it will be readily understood that the task which is set before the nation depends, for its accomplishment, upon the spiritual salvation of each individual member of the nation.

The Fig Tree of Judah

Although only a small part of the tribes of Judah, Benjamin and Levi, the Jews were the official representatives of the whole scattered people of Israel. They had been brought back to their own land especially to receive the Messiah; and on their acceptance of Him as their national Redeemer and personal Saviour, depended their fitness to retain the headship of the Kingdom of God on earth.

Hence the solemn warning of John the Baptist:

146

"Think not to say within yourselves, we have Abraham to our father; for I say unto you that God is able of these stones to raise up children unto Abraham.

"And now also the axe is laid unto the root of the trees; therefore every tree which bringeth not forth good fruit is hewn down, and cast into the fire." Matthew iii, 9-10.

For three years Jesus pleaded with His Father for the Jews. But the Jews, so far from accepting Him, and thus bearing fruit, rejected Him and put Him to death. In crucifying the Lord of Glory they proved their national unfitness for their task; they refused to "bring forth good fruit," so their tree was cursed and cut down; the headship of the Kingdom of God was taken from them and given to a nation which should, in due time, bring forth the fruits of that Kingdom.

Read Luke xiii, 6-9; Matthew xxi, 18-19, 43.

At the same time God did raise up children to Abraham, almost from the very stones, by admitting to the kingdom of Israel, as adopted children, all who should believe on His Son. By His precious death and burial, by His glorious resurrection and ascension, the Son Himself opened the Kingdom of Heaven to all believers.

Read Galatians iii, 26-29; Colossians i, 12-14.

The Tradition of the Elders

Whether John the Baptist foresaw this development or not, it is certain that he had a clear and true perception of the Abrahamic Covenant. Our Lord's emphatic confirmation of his doctrine is sufficient evidence of this.

John saw the Kingdom of Heaven, founded in Abraham, Isaac and Israel, and developed in their descendants, both the minority then in Palestine and the majority who were scattered abroad. In this kingdom he saw a nucleus capable of infinite expansion, through the redemptive power and saving grace of the Holy One of Israel.

The Jewish leaders, on the contrary, desired to seize and retain for themselves all the privileges of the Abrahamic Covenant without undertaking its world-wide responsibilities. This attitude of mind was the direct result of the teaching of the Modernists and Higher Critics of the pre-Christian era, who had distorted the truth of the Scriptures for their own purposes.

So sedulously had the clergy of the Jewish Church misinterpreted and undermined the Written Word of God, and so intoxicated were they with their own cleverness, that they despised the Living Word of God and nailed Him to the cross.

In accordance with prophecy, we are witnessing a recurrence of these phenomena at the present time; and we must beware lest we, too, bring upon ourselves the rebuke of the Master:

"Full well ye reject the commandment of God, that ye may keep your own tradition.

"Making the word of God of none effect through your tradition, which ye have delivered."

Read Mark vii, 9 and 13.

It was tradition which blinded the eyes of the Jews to the Messiah at His first coming, and it is tradition which is blinding the eyes of Israel to-day.

"Thus have ye made the commandments of God of none effect by your tradition.

"Ye hypocrites, well did Esaias prophesy of you, saying, This people draweth nigh unto Me with their mouth, and honoureth Me with their lips; but their heart is far from Me.

"But in vain do they worship Me, teaching for doctrines the commandments of men."

Read Matthew xv, 6-9.

The kingdom of Israel will endure because God has sworn by His holiness that it shall endure, not for the gratification of its own selfish interests, but in order that it may carry out His righteous purposes in the earth.

Nor is the corollary of this great truth any less important. Only by faith in the living Christ can the individual members of that kingdom hope to receive for themselves personal spiritual salvation; and only in the power of that salvation can they hope to weld themselves into a truly Christian nation, eager to fulfil its destiny, and to win the world for the Everlasting King.

CHAPTER XXXV

THE BLINDNESS OF ISRAEL

It is hardly a matter for surprise that the people of the kingdom of Israel should have forgotten their identity. Indeed, it would have been strange had they not done so, for after their deportation to Media they had been broken up into many sections and called by many names. Only after many centuries had the bulk of them been gathered together in the islands of the north-west under a new name.

Read Isaiah lxii, 2.

The Title

The word "Israel" is something more than a name. It is a title which was conferred by God upon Jacob, the ancestor of the Israel race, and means "Ruling with God."

Read Genesis xxxii, 28; Deuteronomy xxviii, 9-10.

In the book of Ezekiel we read of God's long-suffering patience with the Children of Israel. We are told that it was in God's mind to take away the title when they were in Egypt, and later when they were in the wilderness; and we realise that He only refused to allow them to bear His name when there was no longer any hope that they would cease to dishonour it.

The kingdom of Israel, like the kingdom of Judah, broke the Third Commandment. They took, or bore, the name of God in vain; they profaned the name of God. Therefore the title was taken from them by divine decree.

Read Exodus xx, 7; Ezekiel xx, 1-39.

This national blindness is, then, part of Israel's punishment. But inasmuch as all divine punishment has a beneficent purpose, we may suppose that it was imposed for a two-fold object: firstly, to prevent a recurrence of national pride; secondly, to protect the tribes while they were being gathered into the Appointed Place, and while they were being developed into an empire.

The Manifestation of Israel

For the time when this blindness will be removed all the world is waiting, wittingly or unwittingly.

Read Ezekiel xx, 40-44; Isaiah xlii, 16-20; xliii, 1-21; xliv, 1-8.

St. Paul tells us that all Creation is groaning in pain while it waits for the manifestation of the sons of God; while in Hosea we find the Lord's own promise: "In the place where it was said unto them, Ye are not My people, there it shall be said unto them, Ye are the sons of the living God."

Read Romans viii, 18-22; Hosea i, 10.

Dealing further with this point, St. Paul describes the effect on the world of Israel's restoration as "life from the dead," and adds that the partial blindness of Israel must endure until the fulness of the Gentiles be come in.

When we put this statement alongside our Lord's own prediction, "Jerusalem shall be trodden down of the Gentiles, until the times of the Gentiles be fulfilled," we realise that the time has already come when the blindness of Israel must begin to pass away.

Jerusalem was trodden down of the Gentiles until the forces of Israel under Lord Allenby entered the city in 1917. And although Israel has not yet fitted herself to retake her ancient title, the day must be close at hand when the promise of the Lord will be fulfilled:

"Their seed shall be known among the Gentiles, and their offspring among the people; all that see them shall acknowledge them, that they are the seed which the Lord hath blessed."

Read Romans xi, 1-29; Luke xxi, 24; Ezekiel xxxix, 7; xxxix, 21-22; Isaiah lxi, 9.

Chapter XXXVI

THE SECOND ADVENT

(I). PRELIMINARY SIGNS

Events of the future, as revealed in the Bible, form a subject which should be approached with especial care and reverence, bearing in mind that prophecy, in the sense of prediction, is not intended to satisfy vulgar curiosity, but to prove the omniscience, the truth and the faithfulness of God.

Of these future events none has been stated with greater clarity than that of the Second Coming of the Messiah as the Anointed King. It is emphatically proclaimed by the Prophets, by the Apostles, and by our Lord Himself; it is an essential part of the teaching of the whole Bible, and we shall disregard it, or attempt to explain it away, at our peril.

Almost the last words of the Bible are those of the Ascended Christ, "Surely I come quickly." But because that promise has not been redeemed after nearly 2,000 years, our faith has wavered, we have lost our vision, and some of us have already reached that stage of faithlessness which was foreseen by St. Peter.

Read Revelation xxii, 16-20; 2 Peter iii, 1-4.

Because we have lost our faith in that great message of hope, we are witnessing in our churches to-day that "falling away" from true Christianity which was also foretold by St. Paul.

Read 2 Thessalonians ii, 1-4.

The most important testimony concerning the Second Advent is, of course, that which is given to us by our Lord Himself.

Read Luke xxi, 25-36; Mark xiii, 19-27; Matthew xxiv, 21-51.

Nowhere in the Bible is the exact time of the Second Advent revealed. Jesus Himself made the definite statement that it was not known to Him, or to the angels or, indeed, to any one except the Father. But He did foretell certain "signs" which should precede His return, and commanded His disciples to watch for them.

That command applies equally to His disciples of to-day. For to those who are not watching and observing the signs of the times, His Coming will be as sudden as lightning, as unexpected as a thief, and as calamitous as a snare.

The Order of the Signs

It would seem that the Second Advent is a process, consisting of a number of definite events, which follow one another in sequence. And although it should not be assumed that this must necessarily be the case, a comparison of the three Gospel versions would appear to give us the following order:

> False systems of Christianity;
> Infidelity;
> Tribulation;
> Preparations for war;
> War;
> Natural phenomena;
> Earthquake;
> Sign of the Son of Man;
> Coming with great power and glory;
> Trumpet of God;
> Gathering of the elect;
> Occupation of the throne.

These events are confirmed by the Ascended Christ in His Book of Revelation, where the order would seem to be:

> Preparations for war;
> Natural phenomena;
> Earthquake;
> War;
> Gathering of the elect;
> Occupation of the throne.

It will be observed that war seems to precede the natural phenomena and earthquake in the Gospels, and to succeed them in Revelation. From this it may be inferred that these three events are contemporaneous, the natural phenomena and the earthquake actually bringing the war to an end.

Having arrived at a possible sequence of events, we may now try to fill in the details by reading certain passages of Scripture as nearly as possible in the order in which we should expect these events to take place.

False Systems of Christianity

It would be tedious to recount the many false systems of religion which already exist, and which are steadily growing in number. These were predicted by Jesus during His mortal life, foreseen by St. Paul, and revealed by the Ascended Christ to the Apostle John.

Read Matthew xxiv, 23-27; 2 Thessalonians ii, 1-12.
Revelation xvii.

Infidelity

Both our Lord and His Apostles clearly foretold that "falling away," or loss of faith, which would precede the Second Advent. And we are led to understand that this state of infidelity will be brought about, in no small measure, by the doctrine of Evolution, which denies both the Creation and the Fall.

The literal translation of the Greek words $\tau\hat{\omega}$ $\psi\epsilon\acute{v}\delta\epsilon\iota$ in 2 Thessalonians ii, 11, and of $\tau\grave{o}$ $\psi\epsilon\hat{v}\delta o\varsigma$ in John viii, 44, is THE lie.

When, therefore, Jesus states that Satan was a murderer *from the beginning*, and the father of *the* lie, we realise that that falsehood to which He refers is THE LIE by which Satan became the murderer of the whole human race.

From St. Paul's words we gather that the same lie will bring the world to that state of infidelity which was foreseen by Jesus when He cried just before His crucifixion: "Nevertheless, when the Son of Man cometh, shall He find THE FAITH ($\tau\eta\nu$ $\pi\iota\sigma\tau\iota\nu$) upon the earth?"

Read 2 Thessalonians ii, 11; John viii, 42-46; Luke xviii, 8; Matthew xxiv, 11-13.

Tribulation

Although the "time of trouble" which precedes the Second Advent is not entirely economic, the gradual breaking

153

down of the Babylonian system, in preparation for the establishment of the Divine System, must bring in its train considerable perplexity and distress. This will be especially severe for those who, ignorantly or wilfully, attempt to resist the process.

Read Mark xiii, 19-20.

Preparations for War

In the twelfth chapter of the Book of Revelation, the Ascended Christ shows to His Apostle John a vision of a woman "clothed with the sun and the moon under her feet, and upon her head a crown of twelve stars."

The key to the identity of this symbolic woman is given to us in the first book of the Bible. There we read that Joseph dreamed a dream in which the sun and the moon and eleven stars made obeisance to him, and was rebuked by his father Israel, with the words: "Shall I and thy mother and thy brethren indeed come to bow down ourselves to thee to the earth?"

Read Genesis xxxvii, 9-11.

Upon his death-bed in Egypt, Israel bestowed the birth-right upon Joseph, and entailed it to Joseph's younger son Ephraim. The woman, then, represents the people of Israel, led by the tribe of Ephraim.

Having established the identity of the woman, we realise that this chapter contains a rapid survey of one particular phase in the age-long struggle between Good and Evil, between God the Son and Satan.

We are shown the persistent efforts of the Devil to destroy Israel, not only before the birth of Jesus, but up to the present day and, indeed, beyond it; for we learn that Satan, knowing that his time is short, determines in great wrath to make war on those descendants of Israel who have become a Christian nation or nations.

Read Revelation xii.

The Three Unclean Spirits

Satan's chief agents in the preparation of this great campaign are "three unclean spirits like frogs," which

154

issue from the mouths of Satan and of two symbolic figures called the Beast and the False Prophet. These evil spirits incite those nations which are most opposed to the purposes of God, to destroy the Empire which He has prepared for His Son.

Read Revelation xvi, 13-14.

The Peaceable Multitude

Meanwhile the Ten Tribes of Israel have become a "peaceable multitude," with no desire whatever for war. They have, however, allowed themselves to be involved in the Babylonian system, both economically and politically; and for this reason God makes two separate appeals to them to disentangle themselves, promising that if they seek Him with all their heart and soul in the Great Tribulation, He will deliver them.

Read 2 Esdras xiii, 18-53; Isaiah xxvi, 20-21; Revelation xviii, 1-5; Deuteronomy iv, 25-31.

Anti-God Nations

As a result of the flood of evil propaganda which has been inspired by the three unclean spirits, certain nations determine to make war upon Israel, and therefore upon her coming King, God the Son. The heads of these nations are described as ten kings who have the power of kings, but who "have received no kingdom as yet."

While these uncrowned kings may possibly be identified as ten dictators of ten totalitarian states, they undoubtedly correspond with the last extremities of Nebuchadnezzar's image, the ten toes partly iron and partly clay, upon which the Kingdom of the Stone was to fall, crushing the whole of the Babylonian system to powder.

Read Revelation xvii, 12-14.

During His mortal life the Lord Jesus quoted from Psalm cx, and stated that David was speaking of Him as the Messiah when he said: "The Lord (God the Father) said unto my Lord (God the Son) sit Thou on My right hand, until I make Thine enemies Thy footstool." We have, therefore, the very highest authority for saying that this psalm is prophetic of the Second Advent.

Read Matthew xxii, 41-46; Psalm cx.

Psalm ii is also prophetic of the same event. The first three verses describe the crazy conspiracy of the anti-God nations and their leaders. In the next six verses God proclaims His inflexible determination to set up His Son as King over the whole world at Jerusalem. The last three verses contain a solemn warning to the responsible heads of those nations not to incur the wrath of God the Son. The terrible nature of that wrath is portrayed in the Book of Revelation, where the Ascended Christ tells us that one manifestation of it will take the form of the greatest earthquake of all time.

Read Psalm ii; Revelation vi, 12-17.

As we shall see later, the anti-God nations organise themselves into two main expeditions, one of which advances on Palestine from the south, and the other from the north. These expeditions may be acting in concert or in opposition, but the object of both is the same—the capture of the Holy Land and Jerusalem.

Palestine stands at the junction of three continents, and commands the direct waterway from the western to the eastern hemisphere. It is also the birthplace of the three great monotheistic religions of the world, Christianity, Judaism and Islam. In addition to this, the Holy Land is part of the territory which was promised to Abraham, and to which God has sworn that He will gather the outcasts of Israel; while Jerusalem is the future capital of the world-wide Kingdom of God the Son.

By capturing Palestine, then, the anti-God nations hope to accomplish two things. They seek to overthrow and destroy the Kingdom of God on earth; and they intend to prove the non-existence of God or, at any rate, His impotence to protect that land and that city which He has sworn to defend and which He has made so peculiarly His own.

CHAPTER XXXVII

THE SECOND ADVENT

(II). THE BATTLE OF THAT GREAT DAY OF GOD ALMIGHTY

Actual hostilities by land and sea seem to start in the Mediterranean, when a certain "king of the north" advances victoriously through many countries, including Egypt, which he despoils.

At a certain stage in the campaign this personage receives alarming news from the north-east, and in consequence hastens his advance on Jerusalem. Arrived there, he encamps on the Mount of Olives, and lays siege to the city, which he eventually captures and sacks.

Read Daniel xi, 40-45; Zechariah xii, 1-2; xiv, 1-2.

Meanwhile the second expedition is approaching from the north, and the position of the armies of Israel is becoming desperate. Hitherto Israel has been relying more on her own power and might than on the Lord of Hosts, who alone can give the victory; for we hear the voice of God exhorting His people to repent and turn to Him for pardon and deliverance.

Read Joel ii, 12-17.

In this extremity the eyes of Israel are opened to all her sins and shortcomings, and she turns back to the Lord her God with her whole heart.

Read Zechariah xii, 3—xiii.

Immediately upon this national repentance, we again hear the voice of God, this time promising to deliver His people and to remove far off from them the northern army.

Read Joel ii, 18-21; ii, 30-32; Zephaniah iii, 8.

From this time onward the armies of Israel are not engaged, for the conduct of the war is taken out of their hands by God the Son. The battle is the Lord's battle, just as it was in the days of Gideon and Jehoshaphat.

Armageddon

The northern army is allowed to advance as far as a place called Armageddon. This may be the valley of Megiddo, also called the plain of Esdrælon, which stretches in a south-easterly direction from Mount Carmel and the new naval port of Haifa. Here many notable battles have been fought, including that in which God Himself defeated the Midianites and Amalekites, using only Gideon and three hundred men.

In the Book of Joel this place is described as the valley of Jehoshaphat, and also as the valley of decision. Jehoshaphat was king of Judah when God defeated the Moabites and Ammonites without calling upon the men of Judah to loose an arrow or to draw a sword. Moreover, the name Jehoshaphat is a compound of the words "Jehovah" and "shaphat," meaning God the Judge. The valley of Jehoshaphat is therefore the valley of decision, or the place where God will judge the rebellious nations.

From this it would appear that the two names, "Armageddon" and "Valley of Jehoshaphat" may be employed to indicate the nature of the conflict rather than the actual site of the battle. At the same time the place may be the plain of Esdrælon, and this is not unlikely in view of the fact that the destruction of the hosts of Gog takes place upon the mountains of Israel, or in other words, in a region somewhere to the north of Palestine.

Read Ezekiel xxxviii, 1-17; Revelation xvi, 14-16; Joel ii, 9-14; Judges vii, 2 Chronicles xx, 14-17.

Spiritual and Material Forces

The forces employed by the Lord Jesus in this great conflict with Satan are both spiritual and material, and may be set out as below:

Spiritual Forces

The Archangel Michael;
The Hosts of the Lord.

158

Earthquake;
Plague;
Internecine strife;
Overflowing rain;
Hail;
Fire and brimstone.

Michael

The Archangel Michael was the captain of the Hosts of the Lord when Satan tried to usurp the Throne of God. He is also the guardian angel of the Children of Israel. Now, at this time of the end, he stands up with his angels to do battle once more against the Devil and his angels.

Read Revelation xii, 7-9; Daniel xii, 1.

The Hosts of the Lord

Throughout history the Hosts of Heaven have been employed by God to carry out His purposes. Only on the very rarest occasions have they been visible to the human eye, as when they were revealed to Elisha and his servant. In the battle of that great day of God Almighty, these invisible armies will be used again.

Read 2 Kings vi, 15-17; Joel ii, 1-11; Revelation xix, 11-16.

The Earthquake

If we take our thoughts back for a moment to the First Advent of the Lord Jesus, we shall remember that after His resurrection He possessed a body which, although no longer mortal, bore the marks of His crucifixion, and was recognisable, visible and tangible.

Forty days after He had risen from the dead He led His Apostles out of Jerusalem on to the Mount of Olives, and there a cloud received His immortal resurrection body out of their sight.

While their attention was still rivetted on the sky, two angels appeared to the Apostles and said: "Ye men of Galilee, why stand ye gazing up into heaven? This same Jesus, which is taken up from you into heaven, shall so come in like manner as ye have seen Him go into heaven."

In the battle of that great day of God Almighty, Jesus returns just as He went; with the same visible, tangible, but immortal, body, and to the very same place.

Read Acts i, 1-11.

The coming of Jesus to the Mount of Olives is the signal for the greatest earthquake which the world has ever known; and this cataclysm has many consequences. It utterly disorganises the northern army. It splits the Mount of Olives in two parts from north to south; and possibly engulfs the forces of the king of the north, if they are still encamped there. It destroys the Nile Delta and the Gulf of Suez, thus making the Suez Canal a thing of the past. At the same time it opens up a new waterway from the Mediterranean Sea down the Jordan Valley to the Gulf of Akaba, making Jerusalem the greatest and the safest port in the world.

Read Ezekiel xxxviii, 18-20; Revelation vi, 12-17; xvi, 18-20; Zechariah xiv, 3-11; Joel iii, 15-21; Isaiah xi, 15-16.

The Plague

Fatal alike to man and beast the next scourge suggests a corrosive gas of the deadliest kind, which is released by the enemy and turned back upon themselves by a sudden change of wind.

Read Zechariah xiv, 12 and 15.

Internecine Strife

A form of madness descends upon the attacking nations, which causes them to turn their weapons upon each other.

Read Zechariah xiv, 13; Ezekiel xxxviii, 21.

Hail, Rain, Fire and Pestilence

Among the natural forces employed by the Lord Jesus the hail is exceptionally severe.

In what is undoubtedly one of the oldest books of the Bible, the Almighty God asks Job, "Hast thou seen the treasures of the hail which I have reserved against the time of trouble, against the day of battle and war?"

In the last book of the Bible the Ascended Christ reveals the terrible nature of this scourge. If the talent mentioned there is the Attic talent, which was current when St. John wrote the book, each hailstone will weigh about 57 lbs.

Read Ezekiel xxxviii, 22-23; Job xxxviii, 22-23; Revelation xvi, 21.

The utter destruction of the northern army by the Lord Jesus takes place upon the mountains of Israel, which indicates a place somewhere to the north of Palestine. So great is the carnage of men and horses, that all the available population of the country is occupied for seven months in burying the dead; after that time a special corps is created to continue the work. Even the wild beasts and carrion birds are called upon by Almighty God to assist in cleansing the land.

Read Ezekiel xxxix, 1-22; Revelation xix, 17-21.

Thus God defends both His land and His people, and brings all war to an end by the demonstration of His invincible might.

Read Psalm xlvi.

CHAPTER XXXVIII

THE SECOND ADVENT

(III). THE GATHERING OF THE ELECT

Like most phases of the Kingdom of God, the Gathering of the Elect has both a material and a spiritual aspect.

Materially, the Chosen People, that is to say, all racial Israel, is to be gathered into the Kingdom. This we may call the Regathering of Israel and Judah.

Spiritually, all chosen servants of God, of every period, race, and denomination, are to be gathered into the body of the King. This is called in the Bible the First Resurrection.

These two gatherings are separate and distinct events or processes. Both take place apparently after the Great Battle, but no indication is given as to whether one precedes the other in point of time.

L   161

The Regathering of Israel and Judah forms one of the great themes of the Old Testament; the First Resurrection forms one of the great themes of the New Testament. Both are essential to the Kingdom of Jesus, for the saints of the First Resurrection compose His administrative body; while the united race of Israel composes the nucleus of that kingdom which will gradually extend over the whole world.

The Sign of the Son of Man

Our Lord, in warning His disciples not to be deceived by false Christs or false prophets, stated that His Second Coming would be unmistakable; "For as the lightning cometh out of the east, and shineth even unto the west; so shall the coming of the Son of Man be."

These words certainly indicate the suddenness and the brilliance of His Coming; and they may possibly convey some idea of the sign which will appear in the heavens.

At the same time it should be noted that Jesus spoke of His return, not as the Son of God, but as the Son of Man; and we cannot help supposing that He wished to impress upon His disciples that He would come back to this world in the visible, tangible body which He possessed after His resurrection, and in which He ascended into Heaven.

The Trumpet of God, the Shout of the Lord, and the Voice of the Archangel

Just as the Trumpet of God and the Voice of the Lord reverberated over Sinai at the establishment of the Kingdom of God on earth, so the Trumpet of God will ring out again, so the Shout of the Lord and the Voice of the Archangel will thunder once more, when the Kingdom of God is re-established upon the earth with God Himself as King.

Read Matthew xxiv, 27-31.

CHAPTER XXXIX

THE SECOND ADVENT

(IV). THE FIRST RESURRECTION

When the Trumpet of God issues its challenge, and the Shout of the Lord commands, the spirits of those who are dead in Christ rise to meet Him in the air, clothed with new, immortal bodies. Then the mortal bodies of those who are still alive in Christ are changed instantaneously into new, immortal bodies; and they, too, are caught up to meet their Lord in the air.

Read 1 Thessalonians iv, 13-18; 1 Corinthians xv, 51-57.

The Body of Christ

Patriarchs, prophets, apostles, martyrs; those who have given up their lives in the service of Jesus; those who have shown their faith in Him, and their willingness to work for Him; all those individuals of all times, all races, and all classes who have witnessed for Him, are gathered together to share in the administration of His kingdom.

This is called the First Resurrection, as distinct from the general resurrection which takes place at the end of the millennial reign. Blessed indeed will be those faithful servants of the Messiah who are privileged to form His administrative body; "on such the second death hath no power, but they shall be priests of God, and of Christ, and shall reign with Him a thousand years".

Read Luke xiii, 28-30; Revelation xi, 18; xx, 4-6; Matthew xix, 27-30; xxiv, 36-44; Colossians i, 18 and 24.

The Resurrection of the Body

The doctrine of the resurrection of the body is one of the essential articles of the Christian faith. It appears as follows in those three great creeds which have come down to us from the earliest times:

In the Apostles' Creed: "I believe in the resurrection of the body."

In the Nicene Creed: "I look for the resurrection of the dead."

In the Athanasian Creed: "All men shall rise again with their bodies."

All this is, of course, in accordance with the teaching, not only of the New Testament, but also of the Old Testament. Perhaps the most remarkable statement of faith in the resurrection of the body is to be found in Job, which is supposed to be one of the earliest books of the Bible.

"I know that my Redeemer liveth, and that He shall stand at the latter day upon the earth; and though after my skin worms destroy this body, yet in my flesh shall I see God."

Read Job xix, 25-27.

St. Paul's Argument

Yet there have always been those who say, like the Sadducees, that there is no resurrection. When some members of the Church of Corinth fell into this error, St. Paul was at great pains to bring them back to the truth.

With unanswerable logic he argued that if man could not rise from the dead, then the Messiah, who became man, did not rise; and if the Messiah did not rise, then all hope of a future life is vain. If the Christian Gospel is not a hollow mockery, the Messiah did rise from the dead, and has become the first fruits of them that slept; that is to say, He is the first man to rise from the dead and to receive the immortal human body.

Jesus took our fallen nature upon Him; He received the corrupt, dishonoured, weak, mortal body which Adam possessed after his fall.

He put Himself on trial in place of Adam, accepting the handicap of the post-Fall body. He subjected Himself to the same and, indeed, to fiercer temptations. He proved Himself sinless; and being sinless, He was able to offer Himself as a full, perfect and sufficient sacrifice, oblation and satisfaction for the sins of the whole world.

He came to seek and to save that which was lost. He came to redeem the Lost Sheep of the House of Israel, but He came also to save that which was lost by Adam in the

164

Garden of Eden. To quote St. Paul's own words: "Since by man came death, by man came also the resurrection from the dead. For as in Adam all die, even so in Christ shall all be made alive."

By tasting the bitterness of death for every man, Jesus regained for man the original immortal human body, made in the image and likeness of God; or if not only that, then something infinitely more beautiful. He led the way through death to the immortal body; and, in so doing, He became Himself THE WAY to everlasting life.

Read 1 Corinthians xv, 12-23; Romans v, 12-21.

St. Paul then describes the spiritual counterpart of the human body, which is raised from the dead, even after corruption of the mortal counterpart has taken place.

There is, he says, a natural (mortal) body and a spiritual (immortal) body. The mortal body is sown in corruption; it is raised in incorruption. It is sown in dishonour; it is raised in glory. It is sown in weakness; it is raised in power. It is sown a mortal body; it is raised an immortal body.

Read 1 Corinthians xv, 35-50.

The Resurrection Body

From St. John we learn that this spiritual body will be like the body of Jesus; that is to say, it will be like the immortal human body which Jesus possessed after His resurrection, with which He ascended into Heaven, and in which He will again appear at His Second Coming.

Read 1 John iii, 1-2; Acts i, 9-11; Revelation i, 7.

During the forty days which elapsed between His resurrection and ascension, Jesus demonstrated His spiritual body to His disciples. He was still man, but man with the resurrection body.

At first the disciples were terrified, and thought that they had seen a spirit. But Jesus quickly reassured them. "Behold My hands and My feet, that it is I Myself. Handle Me, and see; for a spirit hath not flesh and bones, as ye see Me have."

His body still bore the marks of His crucifixion. Thomas was commanded to put his finger into the prints of the nails, and to thrust his hand into the gash made by the spear.

He walked and talked with His disciples; He even ate with them; He was visible, tangible and recognisable; yet His body was changed. He said He had flesh and bones, and proved it. But He did not mention blood; and this omission, if not accidental, may perhaps supply a clue to the change which took place.

Although He still had the appearance of mortal man, He could pass through stone walls, locked doors, and barred windows; He could conceal His identity; He could appear and disappear at will. He was no longer subject to the limitations of the material; for, as man, He had regained for man that immortal body which man himself had lost.

Read Luke xxiv, 13-43; John xx, 11-31.

The Messiah's Manhood taken into God

Nor was this all. For as man, clothed in the resurrection body, He ascended into Heaven, and resumed His Godhead; thus taking the Manhood into God, and raising it to the highest glory and honour.

The Way to Life

This immortal human body, this free gift of everlasting life, the Lord Jesus offers to all those who consecrate their lives to His service.

As God the Son, the Ascended Messiah has that quality which is called in the Bible "Life-in-Himself"; that is to say, He has life, not by permission, but by inherent right. The power to give life to man has been placed in His hands by the Father, and He can bestow it upon whom He will.

Thus Jesus is, as He claims to be, the Way, the Truth, the Life, and the only means of communion with the Father.

Read Matthew xvi, 24-28; John v, 19-30; xiv, 6.

The Lord's Supper

Self-dedication, however, gives birth to a new spiritual life which must be sustained by spiritual food. The true follower of Jesus must take his Saviour into his very system; he must eat the Bread of Life, which is the body of the Messiah. In the symbols of bread and wine he must eat and drink the spiritual flesh and blood of the Christ, for without this spiritual food he is spiritually hungry and thirsty, and the spiritual life dies within him.

Read John vi, 26-58; Matthew xxvi, 26-28; Mark xiv, 22-24; Luke xxii, 19-20.

Those who are Christ's at His Coming

All true Christians, then, receive this free gift of everlasting life. But the Elect, or Chosen, that is to say, those who are accounted most worthy, receive the new, immortal human body at our Lord's Second Advent, in order that they may share with Him in the administration of His Millennial Kingdom.

To them will be granted the supreme privilege of sitting with the Everlasting King upon the throne of His father David, even as He now sits upon the Throne of God the Father in Heaven.

Read Revelation iii, 20-21; v, 9-10.

CHAPTER XL

THE SECOND ADVENT

(v). THE REGATHERING OF ISRAEL AND JUDAH

Divine utterances of the Old Testament paint a vivid picture of the reunion of all racial Israel in one nation under one king; and this great event is so closely interwoven with the restoration to Jerusalem of the Throne of the Lord over all Israel, that these two subjects must perforce be considered together.

The Parable of the Dry Bones

One very remarkable prophecy concerning the revitalisation of Israel is to be found in the Book of Ezekiel. There the prophet sees a vision of countless bleached bones, scattered over a wide valley. At the command of the Lord these bones come together, bone to his bone, and are covered with sinew, flesh and skin. At a further command the breath of life comes into these bodies, and they stand upon their feet an exceeding great army.

These bones represent the scattered, and spiritually dead, House of Israel, which is brought back to the fulness of life by the outpouring of the Holy Spirit. Just as the Holy Spirit descended upon the disciples of Jesus at the first Pentecost after the Ascension, so the Holy Spirit will be poured out on a large scale at the regathering of Israel into the Kingdom.

Read Ezekiel xxxvii, 1-14; Joel ii, 28-32; Acts ii, 1-21.

The Parables of the Two Sticks

Immediately after the vision of the dry bones, Ezekiel is commanded to take a stick and to write upon it: "For Judah, and for the children of Israel his companions"; then he is commanded to take another stick and to write upon it: "For Joseph, the stick of Ephraim, and for all the house of Israel his companions."

When he has done this, the two sticks join themselves together in one stick; and the Lord tells Ezekiel that He will gather ten-tribed Israel and two-tribed Judah, and unite them in one nation, under one king of the house and lineage of David, who shall be their king for ever.

Reunited and reconstituted as God's own people under the Everlasting King, Israel and Judah come fully under the New Covenant in Christ Jesus; they are purified and cleansed; and the Law of the Lord is written in their very hearts.

Read Ezekiel xxxvii, 15-28; Jeremiah iii, 18; xxxi, 31-34;
Ezekiel xxxvi, 16-38.

The Representative Return to the Holy Land

Palestine, or rather that region between the Nile and the Euphrates which was promised to Abraham, is, of course, the central scene of this great reunion. But inasmuch as that country is far too small for the millions of modern Israel, each of the thirteen tribes will return to the Holy

Land, not as a complete tribe, but representatively, "one of a city and two of a family."

Read Jeremiah iii, 14.

All the prophecies, and they are many, seem to point to the fact that this representative settlement in Palestine will take place after the Battle of That Great Day of God Almighty, and that the culmination of it will be the triumphal entry of Jesus into Jerusalem amid scenes of almost hysterical rejoicing.

Read Ezekiel xxxix, 21-29; Zechariah ii; Zephaniah iii, 14-20; Isaiah xi, 10-13; xl, 9-11; xlii, 12-16; li, 11; Psalm xxiv.

The Bride

Not only are the outlying portions of Israel reunited in one kingdom, but they are also joined together, as of old, under their Divine King.

Beginning with one man and one woman, God had created a nation and a kingdom for Himself; this nation He designed to be, as it were, His partner and helpmeet in carrying out His Great Plan of Salvation; and to this nation, as to a bride, He gave His own name, calling her Israel, which means "Ruling with God."

The Divorce

The bride, however, is unfaithful; she plays the harlot with many lovers (false gods), and for this she is divorced. She bears the name of her Divine Husband in vain; therefore she loses the name of Israel and is driven out into the wilderness of exile.

Read Jeremiah iii, 1-11; iii, 20; Hosea ii, 1-13.

Under the Law of the Lord the unfaithful wife cannot return to her husband; and the Bill of Divorcement which is granted to her under the same Law, can only be blotted out by her husband's death.

Read Isaiah 1, 1; Romans vii, 1-3.

The Redemption

Nevertheless Israel cannot be cast off for ever. Her Lord and Master has made an unconditional covenant with her ancestors which He will not break; and His Great Plan of Salvation cannot be allowed to fail by reason of the sins of His human partner.

Here is a problem in very truth, which only the wisdom and the love of God Himself can solve. How can the Bill of Israel's Divorcement be blotted out when her Husband is immortal? Can God give up His immortality, and die to redeem His bride?

The answer to that question is revealed "by the mouth of God's holy prophets which have been since the world began."

Read Luke i, 67-73; Isaiah liv, 1-10; xliv, 21-23.

The Re-betrothal

When He has sacrificed His own life as the Lamb of God, when He has blotted out the Bill of Divorcement by His death, God the Son woos Israel with His great Gospel of Salvation, and betroths her to Himself again.

Read Hosea ii, 14-23.

The Re-marriage

In the fulness of time the Ascended Christ will return to claim His bride. Then Israel will have been regathered into one nation, with her new centre of government and worship at Jerusalem; she will have been purified, cleansed, and sanctified by the outpouring of the Holy Spirit; she will have arrayed herself in the garments of salvation, and have put on the fine clean white linen which is the righteousness of saints; she will at last have made herself ready to meet her King.

Read Jeremiah iii, 12-17; Isaiah lxi, 10—lxii; Revelation xxi, 9-10; xix, 6-9; Psalm lxviii.

CHAPTER XLI

THE ANOINTED KING

After His ascent into Heaven as the Anointed Priest, the Lord Jesus sat down on the right hand of the Majesty on High, there to wait until the time should come for Him to return to this earth as the Anointed King.

For that great day He bids all His followers to pray continually in the words, "Thy Kingdom come"; for during His millennial reign, the inhabitants of the earth will learn righteousness, and the will of God will be done in this world, even as it is now done in Heaven.

Not only does He command His disciples to pray; He also commands them to watch for the signs of His coming. Those who are praying and watching will not be caught unawares; and they will remember their Master's words: "When ye see these things begin to come to pass, look up and lift up your heads, for your redemption draweth nigh."

The final work of redemption in the millennial reign may be said to present two main aspects, which are complementary and concurrent.

In the first place, Jesus will reign until all His enemies have become His footstool; in other words, He will reign until all the forces of evil have been destroyed.

In the second place, He will complete the "restitution of all things"; that is to say, He will restore all Creation to its original state of perfect harmony with the will of God.

Read Hebrews i, 1-4; x, 12-13; Psalm cx, 1; Acts iii, 19-21; Luke xi, 2; Isaiah xxvi, 9; Luke xxi, 25-28.

Righteousness, Justice and Peace

Having pulverised the war-mongering nations and scattered the advocates of power-politics and brute force, the Messiah, as the Anointed King, takes the throne of His ancestor David, which has been preserved for Him through the centuries.

With His Body, the Saints of the First Resurrection, He

171

reigns primarily over united Israel from the new capital of the Empire at Jerusalem; and one of His first acts will be the restoration to His Kingdom of the Law of the Lord, as amplified by Himself.

Read Isaiah ix, 6-7; xi, 1-5; xxxii, 16-17; xlii, 1-4; li, 1-5; Jeremiah xxiii, 5-8; Luke i, 30-33; Matthew v, 17-20.

So marvellous will be the condition of the Empire under the personal rule of the Messiah, that many of the non-Israel nations will clamour for admission.

All nations, whether admitted into the Empire or not, will be required to send representatives to Jerusalem once a year to worship the King. Those nations which fail to do so will be ruled with "a rod of iron" or, in other words, with the greatest severity. One manifestation of this will be continued drought.

Read Daniel vii, 13-14; Micah iv, 1-8; Zechariah xiv, 16-19; Psalm lxviii, 6; ii, 6-9; Revelation xii, 5; xix, 15; xv, 2-4.

Satan Bound

During this period Satan will be bound and restrained from inciting the inhabitants of the earth to break the Law of the Lord.

Read Revelation xx, 1-3.

The Prince of Peace

Peace, in all its aspects—political, industrial, and individual—will be rigidly enforced. Warfare of all kinds, strikes, lockouts, and personal quarrels will be severely repressed.

Military weapons will be melted down and converted into implements of agriculture. Even the technique of war will be forgotten.

Read Isaiah ii, 4.

The Last Rebellion

By binding Satan, Jesus frees the world from the deception of the Father of Lies; by enforcing the Law of the Lord, He demonstrates that man can only find salvation from evil by obedience to the will of God. But man cannot be saved by compulsion; he must come to his Saviour of his own free will; therefore Satan is released for a little while for the final testing.

Then it is found that even after 1,000 years of government by God the Son Himself, there are still some nations which are willing to listen to the voice of the Tempter. Seeing the Kingdom of God on earth unarmed and apparently defenceless, these nations come up against Jerusalem and are devoured by fire from Heaven.

Read Revelation xx, 7-9; Isaiah lx, 11-12.

Removal of the Curse

With the suppression of this last rebellion all the kingdoms of this world become the Kingdom of the Lord and of His Anointed One. But the Messiah must reign until all His enemies have become His footstool; and these enemies are not only material, but spiritual.

Read Revelation xi, 15; Ephesians vi, 10-13.

During His reign the Saviour has been purging out of His Kingdom all things which offend, and reversing the curse which was brought upon all Creation by the disobedience of Adam.

Read Matthew xiii, 36-43; Genesis iii, 17-18; Romans viii, 22-23.

No longer does the land bring forth thorns and thistles; no longer do the dumb creatures prey upon one another.

Read Isaiah lv, 12-13; xi, 6-9; lxv, 25.

The law of heredity has ceased to operate; disease and sickness have almost disappeared; and in consequence life has been greatly prolonged.

Read Jeremiah xxxi, 29-30; Ezekiel xviii, 1-4; Isaiah lxv, 20.

The Second Resurrection

When this stage has been reached, all the dead are raised to life and judged every one according to his works. We are not told that the judgment follows immediately upon the resurrection, and there may possibly be yet another interval for repentance in the full light of knowledge.

In any event, we may be permitted to hope that there will be very few who persist in rejecting their Saviour, and who follow Satan to their doom.

Read Revelation xx, 10-15; xxi, 6-8.

The Era of Perfection

With the destruction of Satan, and Hell, and Death, all the enemies of Jesus have been vanquished; the Adamic Curse has been finally wiped out; and we enter upon the Era of Perfection.

Read Revelation xxii, 1-5.

In the Kingdom of Jesus, made perfect by His grace, there is no more evil and sin; no more want and hunger; no more poverty and distress; no more sickness and pain; no more bereavement and sorrow; but only happiness, and joy, and peace in the service of the King of kings.

Read Isaiah xlix, 10; Revelation vii, 9-17; xxi, 3-4; 1 Corinthians xv, 24-28.

The age-long fight between Jesus and Satan for the souls of men is finished; the Kingdom is delivered up to the Father that He may be all in all; and the triumph of God's Great Plan of Salvation is complete.

"Blessed be the Lord God, the God of Israel, who only doeth wondrous things. And blessed be His glorious name for ever; and let the whole earth be filled with His glory. Amen and amen."

Read Psalm lxxii.

FURTHER READING

The Covenants of the Bible by R.G.F. Waddington

The Early British Church by L.G. Roberts

Did our Lord visit Britain by C.C. Dobson

The Master Plan by A.S. Gaunt

The Lost Tribes of Israel by Reader Harris

All books from Covenant Publishing